A Touch of Class

QUOTES FOR TEACHERS

COMPILED BY
CAROL VANDERHEYDEN

PHOTOGRAPHS BY CAROL VANDERHEYDEN

Copyright © 2023 Carol VanderHeyden.

All rights reserved. No part of this book may be reproduced, stored, or transmitted by any means—whether auditory, graphic, mechanical, or electronic—without written permission of both publisher and author, except in the case of brief excerpts used in critical articles and reviews. Unauthorized reproduction of any part of this work is illegal and is punishable by law.

The book cover was designed and painted by Stephanie Sodel, who is visually impaired, but has not allowed her disability to prevent her from creating wonderful works of art. Sodel lives in Central Florida with her husband and teaches watercolor classes at Solivita.

ISBN: 979-8-89031-739-1 (sc)
ISBN: 979-8-89031-740-7 (hc)
ISBN: 979-8-89031-741-4 (e)

Because of the dynamic nature of the Internet, any web addresses or links contained in this book may have changed since publication and may no longer be valid. The views expressed in this work are solely those of the author and do not necessarily reflect the views of the publisher, and the publisher hereby disclaims any responsibility for them.

THE EWINGS PUBLISHING

One Galleria Blvd., Suite 1900, Metairie, LA 70001
(504) 702-6708

Dedication

A TOUCH OF CLASS, is dedicated to all the unsung heroes in the teaching profession. Teachers rarely get the recognition or appreciation they deserve for the countless hours of preparation and clerical work they render after hours, or for the hundreds of dollars they spend in out-of-pocket donations for supplies and materials for their classrooms and students. They genuinely care about our nation's children and their futures. These talented and learned professionals are our sport's heroes and deserve similar reparations. When we support our educators as they deserve, we will be a better society and they will get the respect and honor they so merit. The word "Teacher" was used in describing, Jesus, the greatest teacher of all times. What an honor it should be, to be called Teacher, with the responsibility, dignity, prestige, and respect that word entails.

Introduction

This book is a collection of quotations and documents, which I have gathered and used in my classroom over the duration of my thirty-year teaching career. In many ways they are the essence of my teaching and learning experiences in public education.

My retirement from the classroom has brought me the freedom to pursue another dream. I have found great satisfaction and excitement in writing. If my writing achieves its purpose then I have embarked on a second career. It is my desire that this book will be a great resource for teachers.

I used quotes as a cognitive and memorable part of my student's daily educational experience. Asking the questions; what does this quote mean or what is the author trying to communicate with us, will help students to analysis the quote and put it into their own words. Many interesting, spontaneous and enlightening discussions may follow as students share their interpretations. The art of deciphering quotes and writing interpretations is a classy way to start your day, hence the title; A Touch of Class.

The discipline of using meaningful quotes to teach life-lessons in my classroom was met with personal success. Therefore, it is my wish to inspire other teachers to use quotes as a practical part of their classroom experience. Through the implementation of quotes, it is my hope that you and your students will gain insight into the mystery of human behavior and pursue the enrichment of character-building within the class setting.

I have compiled this collection of quotes and documents into three sections: A Wealth of Wisdom for Teachers, The Making of a Great Nation, and Earth's Wonders and Resources. These sections are designed for teachers of all grade levels. In Parts Two and Three, topics related to history and science are emphasized respectively. This treasure of quotes is designed to be a continuous source of strength, encouragement, joy, and enrichment throughout your teaching career.

The Author's Wish for You
May you get all your wishes but one;
So you always have something to strive for.

Contents

PART ONE
A WEALTH OF WISDOM FOR TEACHERS

Chapter 1	Teachers/Educators	3
Chapter 2	Education/Learning	19
Chapter 3	Schools/Students/Parents	37
Chapter 4	Management/Control/Discipline	53
Chapter 5	Potential/Motivation/Inspiration	61
Chapter 6	Wisdom/Knowledge	71
Chapter 7	Careers/Jobs/Work	87

PART TWO
THE MAKING OF A GREAT NATION

Chapter 1	America/U.S.A.	97
Chapter 2	Democracy/Politics/Government	101
Chapter 3	Liberty/Freedom	107
Chapter 4	Citizen/Patriot	113
Chapter 5	Religious Origins/Roots	117
Chapter 6	War/Peace	125
Chapter 7	Historical Documents/Records	135

PART THREE
EARTH'S WONDERS AND RESOURCES

Chapter 1	Animal Kingdom	145
Chapter 2	Earth's Resources	149
Chapter 3	Nature's Gifts	153
Chapter 4	Plant Kingdom	157
Chapter 5	Seasons of the Year	163
Chapter 6	Astronomy	167
Chapter 7	Water Resources	171
Chapter 8	Weather Lore - Meteorology	175

Preface

THE IDEAS I STAND FOR ARE NOT MINE.
I BORROWED THEM FROM SOCRATES.
I SWIPED THEM FROM CHESTERFIELD.
I TOOK THEM FROM JESUS.
AND I PUT THEM IN A BOOK.
IF YOU DON'T LIKE THEIR RULES,
WHOSE WOULD YOU USE?
DALE CARNEGIE

PART ONE

A WEALTH OF WISDOM FOR TEACHERS

WHILE I TEACH, I LEARN.
O'HENRY

Chapter 1

TO BE A TEACHER IS TO WEAR MANY HATS.
ANONYMOUS

Teachers Give Gifts
To the difficult student, Patience
To the quiet student, Assurance
To all students, A Good Example
To parents, Time to Listen
To administrators, Creativity
To the community, Service
To yourself, Respect

Teachers plant the seeds of learning.

Everyday is a new beginning; every morn is the world made new.

Teachers broadcast facts every day Not knowing how many receivers they reach.

A farmer can plow under his mistakes But a teacher's mistakes grow up and become members of the school board.

Goals are like stars; they may not be reached, but they can always be a guide.

All work and little pay means you're a teacher.

Praise is habit forming.

A teacher must strive to teach ideas as well as facts.

Many children have photographic minds; they need the teacher's help to develop them.

A sleeping fox catches no chickens.

Teachers who put their foot down will find their students reluctant to step on their toes.

Criticism: the thing most of us think is more blessed to give than to receive.

Sometimes you can make a very effective statement simply by saying nothing.

Experience is what helps you to recognize a mistake when you've made it again.

What students want to learn is as important as what educators want to teach.

Tact is the art of making a point without making an enemy.

Kindness is the overflowing of one's self into the lives of others.

Give credit where credit is due.

We protest against unjust criticism, but we accept unearned applause.

Today's assignment: Help fight truth decay.

The first fifteen seconds of a lecture will make or break it.

The most valuable gift a teacher can give his students is a good example.

Teaching isn't a bowl of cherries, it's a bunch of raisins - raisin' curiosity, raisin' awareness, and raisin' grades.

Most educators agree that students learn exactly as much in school as they are compelled to learn.

A teacher affects eternity; he can never tell where his influence stops.
    Henry Brooks Adams

Sometimes one teacher can make all the difference:
The teacher who stays after school to help you understand an algebra problem.
The coach who tells you, you can do it- and gets you to run faster than you have ever run before.

Everyone who remembers his own educational experience remembers teachers not methods and techniques.
    Sidney Hook

What constitutes the teacher is the passion to make scholars.
    George Herbert Palmer

Teachers believe they have a gift for giving; it drives them with the same irrepressible drive that drives others to create a work of art or a market or a building.
    A. Barlett Giamatti

I was still learning when I taught my last class.
    Claude M. Fuess (after 40 yrs. of teaching)

My heart is singing for joy this morning. A miracle has happened! The light of understanding has shone upon my little pupil's mind, and behold, all things are changed!
    Annie Sullivan

Enthusiasm finds the opportunities and energy makes the most of them.
    Henry Haskins

Heroes are people who do what has to be done when it needs to be done, regardless of the consequences.

Happiness is contagious - Be a carrier.

Laughter is the corrective force, which prevents us from becoming cranks.
    Henry Bergson

A vacation is what you take when you can no longer take what you've been taking.
    Earl Wilson

Give others a piece of your heart, not a piece of your mind.

What a man does for himself dies with him. What he does for his community lives long after he is gone.
    Theodore Roosevelt

To teach is to learn. Japanese Proverb

It is the supreme art of the teacher to awaken joy in creative expression and knowledge.
    Albert Einstein

My joy in learning is partly that it enables me to teach.
    Seneca

When a teacher calls a boy by his entire name, it means trouble.
    Mark Twain

Teacher: The child's third parent.
    Hyman Maxwell Berston

The most extraordinary thing about a really good teacher is that he or she transcends accepted educational methods.
    Margaret Mead

Retirement means less money and more spouse.

To be persuasive, we must be believable;
to be believable, we must be credible;
to be credible, we must be truthful.
    Edward R. Murrow

Indecision is the worst enemy of creativity.

The good teacher makes the poor student good and the good student superior. When our students fail, we, as teachers, too, have failed.
    Marva Collins

Teachers are expected to reach unattainable goals with inadequate tools. The miracle is that at times they accomplish this impossible task.
    Haim G. Ginot

Teaching is the royal road to learning.
    Jessamyn West

Teaching is the hardest work I've ever done.
    Ann Richards

One may receive the information, but miss the teaching.
    Jean Toomer

Teachers are more than any other classes the guardians of civilization.
    Bertrand Russell

Give a man a fish and you feed him for a day. Teach a man to fish and you feed him for a lifetime.
    Chinese Proverb

Good teaching is one-fourth preparation and three-fourths theater.
    Gail Godwin

By learning you will teach; by teaching you will learn.
    Latin Proverb

A teacher must believe in the value and interest of his subject as a doctor believes in health.
    Gilbert Highet

Teacher: Two kinds:
The kind that fill you with so much quail shot that you can't move, and the kind that just give you a little prod behind and you jump to the skies.
    Robert Frost

A teacher is better than two books.
    German Proverb

The mediocre teacher tells.
The good teacher explains.
The superior teacher demonstrates.
The great teacher inspires.
    William Arthur Ward

A good teacher, like a good entertainer, first must hold his audience's attention. Then he can teach his lesson.
    John Hendrik Clarke

I touch the future. I teach.
    Christa McAuliffe

Self-doubt seems very much a part of the job of teaching: one can never be sure how well it is going.
    Joseph Epstein

The teacher's life should have three periods - study until twenty-five, investigation until forty, profession until sixty, at which age I would have him retired on a double allowance.
    Sir William Osler

Good teachers are glad when a term begins and a little sad when it ends. They remember some of their students for many years, and their students remember them.
    Margaret Mead

The job of a teacher is to excite in the young a boundless sense of curiosity about life, so that the growing child shall come to apprehend it with an excite- ment tempered by awe and wonder.
    John Garrett

To teach is to touch lives forever.

The whole art of teaching is only the art of awakening the natural curiosity of young minds for the purpose of satisfying it afterwards.
    Anatole France

The first idea that the child must acquire in order to be actively disciplined is that of the difference between good and evil: the task of the educator lies in seeing that the child does not confound good with immobility, and evil with activity.
    Maria Montessori

The art of teaching is the art of assisting discovery.
    Mark Van Doren

The object of teaching a child is to enable him to get along without a teacher.
    Elbert Hubbard

A life that hasn't a definite plan is likely to become driftwood.
    David Sarnoff

To teach is to learn twice.
    Joseph Joubert

Teach young people how to think not what to think.
    Sidney Sugarman

Teaching kids to count is fine, but teaching them what counts is best.
    Bob Talbert

Fifty years ago teachers said their top discipline problems were talking, chewing gum, making noise, and running in the halls. The current list, by contrast, sounds like a cross between a rap sheet and the seven deadly sins.
    Anna Quindlen

One good teacher in a lifetime may sometimes change a delinquent into a solid citizen.
    Philip Wylie

I owe a lot to my teachers and mean to pay them back someday.
    Stephen Leacock

A good teacher is one who says something you won't understand until ten years later.
    Julius Lester

Good teachers are costly, but bad teachers cost more.
    Bob Talbert

Most of us end up with no more than five or six people who remember us. Teachers have thousands of people who remember them for the rest of their lives.
    Andrew A. Rooney

The gift of teaching is a peculiar talent, and implies a need and a craving in the teacher himself.
    John Jay Chapman

A successful teacher needs: the education of a college president, the executive ability of a financier, the humility of a deacon, the adaptability of a chameleon, the hope of an optimist, the courage of a hero, the wisdom of a serpent, the gentleness of a dove, the patience of Job, the grace of God, and the persistence of the devil.

If the heavens were a parchment, and the trees of the forest all pens, and every human being were a scribe, it would still be impossible to record all that I have learned from my teachers.
    Jochanan Ben Zakkai

When a teacher deals with a child, she deals with his parents as well.
    Dr. L. A. Duggins

A load of books does not equal one good teacher.
    Ancient Chinese Proverb

No bubble is so iridescent or floats longer than that blown by the successful teacher.
    Harvey Cushing

The best teacher . . . is not one who knows most, but the one who is most capable of reducing knowledge to that simple compound of the obvious and the wonderful which slips into the infantile comprehension.
    H. L. Mencken

You cannot teach a man anything; you can only help him to find it within himself.
    Galileo

Our government is the potent, the omnipresent teacher. For good or for ill, it teaches the whole people by its example.
    McVeigh

A teacher who can arouse a feeling for one single good action, for one single good poem, accomplishes more than he who fills our memory with rows on rows of natural objects, classified with name and form.
    Goethe

The eggs do not teach the hen.
    Russian Proverb

Let nature be your teacher, she has a world of ready wealth . . .
    William Wordsworth

Old teachers never die, they just grade away.
    Henny Youngman

The school kids in some towns are getting so tough that teachers are playing hooky.
    E. C. McHenzie

When ask to give two reasons for entering the teaching profession. The teacher wrote, "July and August."
    Milton Berle

Teachers should petition for higher salaries in August. Parents would give them anything they asked for on the first ballot!
    Bennett Cerf

A Minneapolis high school teacher wrote this sign under the clock in her classroom: "Time will pass . . . will you?"
    James E. Myers

A teacher is a person who used to think he liked children.
    Joey Adams

Enthusiasm is caught not taught.

The substitute teacher has just two rules we have to follow. "Sit down and shut up."
    Mark McGinnis

I am not authorized to fire substitute teachers. I am not authorized to fire . . .
    Bart Simpson

Teaching has ruined more American novelists than drink.
    Gore Vidal

A teacher's constant task is to take a roomful of live wires and see to it that they're grounded.
    E. C. McKenzie

It is when the gods hate a man with uncommon abhorrence that they drive him into the profession of a school-master.
    Seneca

When you wish to instruct, be brief; every word that is unnecessary only pours over the side of the brimming mind.
    Cicero

The secret of teaching is to appear to have known all your life what you learned this afternoon.

If you keep doing what you've always done, you'll keep getting what you've always gotten.

It's extremely difficult to lead further than you have gone yourself.

Hold yourself responsible for a higher standard than anyone else expects of you.
    Henry Ward Beecher

As a general rule, teachers teach more by what they are than by what they say.

Teaching is not a lost art, but the regard for it is a lost tradition.
    Jacques Barzun

Leadership is the power to evoke the right response in other people.
    Humphrey Mynors

A good leader takes a little more than her share of the blame, a little less than her share of credit.

Another reason why experience is the best teacher is because it is always on the job.

Every teacher should realize the dignity of his calling.
    John Dewey

Today, teachers are under tremendous pressure to perform within ever more difficult constraints. Classes are larger, parental participation is not always evident, and students generally have more complex problems and less respect for authority.
    Greg Henry Quinn

Trust is the single most important factor in both personal and professional relationships.

Experience is the best teacher.

Teaching is the greatest of all professions. Only by studying the sciences, developing sensitivity for the arts, and learning the histories can a people progress beyond themselves.
    Greg Henry Quinn

Example is the best way of influencing others.

Experience they say is the best teacher, and considering what it costs, it should be.

The business of a leader is to turn obstacles into stepping-stones, weakness into strength, and disaster into triumph.

A good leader inspires men to have confidence in him; a great leader inspires them to have confidence in themselves.

The world seldom notices who the teachers are, but civilization depends on what they do and what they say.

We can not shine if we have not taken time to fill our lamps.

Few have more opportunities to be heroes than do teachers.
    Greg Henry Quinn

To be a teacher is to wear many hats. A smile increases your face value.

Objectives are often not accomplished because they are not clearly defined and identified.

A professor can never better distinguish himself in his work than by encouraging a clever pupil, for the true discoverers are among them, as comets amongst the stars.
    Carolus Linnaeus

Teachers have a lot of class.

Only the one who serves is qualified to lead.

We judge ourselves by what we feel capable of doing, while others judge us by what we have already done.
    Henry Wadsworth Longfellow

'Excellent,' I cried. 'Elementary,' said he.
    Sir Arthur Conan Doyle

May all your troubles be little ones. We boil at different degrees.
    Julius Caesar

Never a tear bedims the eye
That time, and patience will not dry.
    Bret Harte

Waste of wealth is sometimes retrieved; waste of health, seldom; but waste of time, never.
    Thomas Campion

People populate the world. Teachers civilize it.
    Greg Henry Quinn

He has a right to criticize who has a heart to help.
    Abraham Lincoln

In my experience, the best creative work is never done when one is unhappy.
Albert Einstein Excitement is contagious. I can live for two months on a good compliment.
    Mark Twain

All change represents loss of some kind; that's why some of us resist it so strongly.

Consider how hard it is to change your- self and you'll understand what little chance you have of trying to change others.
    Jacob M. Braude

Be like a duck - keep calm and unruffled on the surface, but paddle like crazy underneath.

Assume cheerfulness you do not feel and shortly you will feel the cheerful- ness you assumed.

Creativity is so delicate a flower that praises tends to make it bloom, while discouragement often nips it in the bud. Any of us will put out more and better ideas if our efforts are truly appreciated.
    Alexander Osborn

Both enthusiasm and pessimism are contagious. Which one do you spread?

Example is not the main thing in influencing others. It is the only thing.
    Albert Schweitzer

I have but one lamp by which my feet are guided, and that is the lamp of experience.
    Patrick Henry

I hear and I forget. I see and I remember. I do and I understand.

To teach a man how he may learn to grow independently, and for himself, is perhaps the greatest service that one man can do for another.
    Benjamin Jowett

If anything goes bad, I did it.
If anything goes semi-good, then we did it. If anything goes real good, then you did it.
    Bear Bryant

The ideas I stand for are not mine. I borrowed them from Socrates. I swiped them from Chesterfield. I took them from Jesus. And I put them in a book. If you don't like their rules, whose would you use?
    Dale Carnegie

I don't know the key to success, but the key to failure is trying to please every- body.
    Bill Cosby

Failure is a far better teacher than success, but she hardly ever finds any apples on her desk.

You cannot help men permanently by doing for them what they could and should do for themselves.
    Abraham Lincoln

Good humor makes all things tolerable.
    Henry Ward Beecher

It is easier to catch flies with honey than with vinegar.

It is too bad that the people who really know how to run the country are busy teaching school.

Often-praised children become more intelligent than often-blamed ones. There's a creative element in praise.
    Thomas Dreier

Praise like gold and diamonds, owes its value to its scarcity.

You can always tell luck from ability by its duration.

I am responsible for my choices and my behaviors. There are no excuses.
I do what I do because it is right. There are no other choices.
I act to create my personal quality world. I am proud of what I want.
I am a leader. I constantly influence. I am no longer powerless.
I am compelled to act on and through "profound knowledge." It is my claim to professionalism.

For every person who wants to teach there are approximately thirty who don't want to learn - much.
    W. C. Sellar and R. J. Yeatman

Children are unpredictable. You never know what inconsistency they're going to catch you in next.

The only reason I always try to meet and know the parents better is because it helps me to forgive the children.
    Louis Johannot

Whatever is worth doing at all, is worth doing well.
    Lord Chesterfield

Punctuality is the politeness of kings and the duty of gentle peoples everywhere.

Be the goal your students aspire to.

Poise is the art of raising the eyebrows instead of the roof.

Candor is always a double-edged sword; it may heal or it may separate.
    Dr. Wilhelm Steke

Passing the Buck . . . Backwards
College Professor:
Such rawness in a student is a shame.
Poor high school preparation is to blame.
High School Principal:
It's plain to see the boy's a fool! The fault's, of course, with grammar school.
Grammar Teacher:
Would from such a dolt I might be spared; they send them up to me so unprepared!
Primary Teacher:
Poor kindergarten child! And they call that preparation? It's worse than none at all!
Kindergarten Teacher:
Never such a lack of training did I see! What sort of person can that mother be!
Mother:

Sometimes a noble failure serves the world as faithfully as a distinguished success.

Difficulties strengthen the mind, as labor does the body.

One picture is worth a thousand words.

Mastery in any art comes only with long practice.

If at first you don't succeed, try, try again.

If at first you don't succeed, try something harder.

Experience is what makes you wonder how it got a reputation for being the best teacher.

A little more determination,
  A little more pluck
A little more work -
  That's LUCK.

Persistency attracts confidence, more than talents and accomplishments.
    E. P. Whipple

What we have to learn to do, we learn by doing.
    Aristotle

It is contact with others which teaches man all he knows.
    Euripides

The purpose of criticism is to help, not to humiliate.

Enthusiasm and success go together.

Most people resist change and it's the only thing that brings progress.

It's just as important to forget a wrong as it is to remember a kindness.

It's impossible to teach without learning something yourself.

The trip is often more fun than the destination.

Do you ever notice that when you are in a big hurry, the person in front of you isn't?

Fame is written in ice and eventually the sun comes out.

To get the right answer, you have to ask the right question.

Respect must be earned.

You never get rewarded for the things you intended to do.

People are more influenced by how much I care than by how much I know.

I am easy to please but difficult to satisfy.

Patience is not passive; on the contrary it is active; it is concentrated strength.

Talent knows what to do; tact knows when and how to do it.

Patience is a tree whose root is bitter, but its fruit is very sweet.

When a happy person enters the room, it's as if another candle had been lighted.

People, who fly into a rage, always make a bad landing.

It is the difficult child that inspires creative teaching.

An automobile needs a driver; a classroom community needs a motivator.

The teacher is the key to motivation; then she will get much more mileage from the class.

Children are most interested in those who are interested in them.

You must be a good manager to be a good leader.

All teachers teach history to those who will make history.

Trust your instincts.

Constant encouragement breeds ambition; constant criticism breeds despair.

Constructive criticism is an oxymoron.

Teaching is what you do, learning is what students achieve, and a better world is what is accomplished for all.

Everything that is taught was discovered, created, accomplished, or improved by someone before.

Without an audience, the song is never as sweet.

Without appreciation, the value of what we do is diminished.

The framework of a successful community is its rules.

Rules must be clear, fair, universal cover all anticipated situations, and there must be a rule for situations that aren't covered.

A caring teacher hands children their passport to the future.
    Jenlane Gee

Practicing courtesy is the stepladder to respect.

Teachers are the wagon masters for the pioneers of the future.

Nothing is more exciting than the prospect of something new.

Winning isn't everything . . . but wanting to win is.
    Vince Lombardi

Teachers are the architectural designers of nations. People must see that education is not an expense, but an investment.
    Donna Oliver

Respect for others is born of self-respect. First, teach children of their own value. Then they will understand the value of others.

If you are to catch the student's interest, excite their appetites.

In teaching you see the results of your success daily. The rewards are often immediate.

For teachers, it is better to get questions than answers. Asking questions is the prerequisite for learning.

The results of patience and repetition are always predictable.

We can do anything we want to if we stick to it long enough.

Men do not fail; they give up trying. While I teach, I learn.
    O. Henry

Old teachers never die; they just fail to make the grade.

Coming together is a beginning, keeping together is progress, and working together is success.
    Henry Ford

In each man is a spark able to kindle new fires of human progress, new light for the human spirit.
    Charles A. Lindbergh

When we do the best we can, we never know what miracle is wrought in our life, or in the life of another.
    Helen Keller

The heritage of the past is the seed that brings forth the harvest of the future.
    Archives Bldg, Washington, D. C.

The Past is my Heritage
The Present is my Responsibility
The Future is my Challenge.

There's only one way to make dreams come true - Wake up and go to work.

Of all the things to wear, your expression is the most important.

I leave this rule for others when I'm dead, Be always sure you're right . . . then go ahead.
    David Crockett

There are two ways of spreading light:
To be the candle or the mirror that reflects it.
    Edith Wharton

How far that little candle throws his beams! So shines a good dead in a naughty world.
    William Shakespeare

Hitch your wagon to a star.
    Ralph Waldo Emerson

Youth must strive for goals afar,
Which old men dare not try.

It is not what you have that matters,
It is what you do with what you have.

It is easier to derail a runaway train than to stop it.

Each defeat makes us weaker for the next battle, but each conquest makes us stronger.

A life that hasn't a definite plan is likely to become driftwood.
    David Sarnoff

The only thing we have to fear is fear itself.
    Franklin D. Roosevelt

Courage is the first of human qualities because it is the quality, which guarantees all the others.
    Winston Churchill

The human race is divided into two classes - those that go ahead and do something and those who sit still and inquire why it wasn't done the other way.
    Oliver Wendell Holmes

Keep your face to the sunshine and you cannot see the shadow.
    Helen Keller

I ask but this, that whenever a thing is right it take no courage to do it, that whenever a thing be wrong, it may have no power of temptation over me.

What you do not start You do not finish.

You give but little when you give of your possessions. It is when you give of yourself that you truly give.
    Gahil Gibran

No man needs sympathy because he has to work . . . Far and away the best prize that life has to offer is the chance to work hard at work worth doing.
    Theodore Roosevelt

Talent knows what to do, Tact knows when to do it.

One of the tests of leadership is the ability to recognize a problem before it becomes an emergency.
    Arnold H. Glasow

A liberal education is at the heart of a civil society, and at the heart of a liberal education is the act of teaching.
    A. Bartlett Giamatti

What office is there which involves more responsibility, which requires more qualifications, and which ought, therefore, to be more honorable, than that of teaching.
    Harriet Martineau

The most secure people offer to share the knowledge of their success and their successes multiply. The insecure will take their secrets to the grave intact.

I have not taught until my pupils have learned.
    Dr. Henrietta Mears

A teacher's dream; A student eager to learn, dedicated and conscious that he is one of a privileged few to receive the benefits of an education.

The essence of good teaching is repetition.

The battle cry of the pessimist is,
"It won't work!"

Nothing is as contagious as optimism.
It rubs off as inspiration, and encouragement
to less daring souls.

We must see each student as a person, not
part of the class data.

T telling and retelling what you have
   studied
E expecting pupils to absorb
A asking and amplifying until facts are clear
C challenging by enthusiasm and genuine
   interest
H hoping never despairing of student
   possibilities
I ingenuity, inventiveness to inspire pupils
N nailing down principles by example
G giving yourself with your ability to teach

Fifty years from now it will not matter what
kind of car you drove, what kind of house
you lived in, how much you had in your bank
account, or what your clothes looked like.
But the world may be a little better because
you were important in the life of a child.

There was never a person who did anything
worth doing that did not receive more than
he gave.
Henry Ward Beecher

The seed can only propagate if it is planted,
watered, and cared for.

We have forty million reasons for failure, but
not a single excuse.
Rudyard Kipling

Be kind to me. Good teachers are hard to
find.

A conference is a meeting at which people
talk about things they should be doing.

Old mathematics teachers never die,
they just reduce to lowest terms.

Good-bye tension, hello pension!
    Retiring teacher, Fay Michaud

Chapter 2

**EDUCATION IS A MEANS TO SOLVING PROBLEMS,
A HANDMAIDEN TO CONSTRUCTIVE CITIZENSHIP,
AN END IN ITSELF, AND AN OBJECT WORTHY OF
PUBLIC SUPPORT FOR ALL OF THESE REASONS.
THOMAS JEFFERSON**

An education is what you get from reading the fine print; a learning experience is what you get when you don't.

By failing to prepare; you are preparing to fail.

Wise men learn by other men's mistakes; fools by their own.

The greatest ability is dependability.
    Curt Bergwall

The best cure for a sluggish mind is to disturb its routine.
    William H. Danford

Learning from experience is like taking the test before the lesson has been presented.

Education does not end upon graduation. It ends when you do.

An educated person has been taught how to think rather than what to think.

A shallow thinker never leaves an impression.

The goal of education should be to turn the mind into a living fountain, not a reservoir.

To understand the value of a year, ask a student who has failed.

It is less painful to learn in our youth than it is to be ignorant in our old age.

To some, education is a tax supported childcare service.

Accentuate the positive, eliminate the negative.
    Johnny Mercer

There is no point in making mistakes if you don't learn anything from them.

You know it's time for a geography lesson when the students claim they cannot find the English Channel on TV.

Some students drink at the fountain of knowledge. Others just gargle.

Some minds are like concrete; thoroughly mixed and permanently set.

Laziness travels so slowly that poverty soon overtakes him.

Ability is nothing without opportunity.
    Napoleon

The seeds of knowledge are planted in the classroom and are cultivated by experience.

Sometimes we think we have an open mind when it really has been closed for repairs.

One must come out of one's house to begin learning.
    African Proverb

If you have knowledge, let others light their candles by it.

Think all you speak, but speak not all you think.

It is the mind that rules the body. Sojourner Truth

Curiosity is the spark, which lights the lamp of learning.

Where there is an inquisitive mind there will always be a frontier.

Repetition impresses a fact indelibly on the mind.

Our education is what remains when we have forgotten all we have been taught.

Genius is one per cent inspiration and ninety-nine per cent perspiration.
    Thomas A. Edison

Knowledge makes men humble, and true genius is ever modest.

No person can ever be a complete failure, for he may serve as an example to others.

A word aptly spoken is like apples of gold in settings of silver.
    Proverbs 25:11

Careful painstaking effort pays in the long run.

Behold the turtle: He makes progress only when he sticks his neck out.
    James Bryant Conant

The highest reward for man's toil is not what he gets for it but what he becomes by it.
    John Ruskin

No man's knowledge here can go beyond his experience.
    John Locke

Haste makes waste.

If your mind becomes too busy, your heart can't respond.

Character development is a primary goal of education.

The dual purposes of education: to inspire and to inform.

The highest tuition paid in the world is to the school of hard-knocks.

A college education is supposed to prepare you for a job, not entitle you to one.

Much learning occurs when the ears are working and the mouth is not.

They think too little that talk too much.

Success and failure are not necessarily final.

There are two kinds of education: One is given to us, the other we give to ourselves.

Communication is the river; understanding is the ocean.
    Greg Henry Quinn

Learning without thought is labor lost; thought without learning is perilous.
    Confucius

The highest result of education is tolerance.
    Helen Keller

Education begins at home. You can't blame schools for not putting into your child what you don't put into him.
    Geoffrey Hold

Anxiety is one of the greatest obstacles and comes in many fashions from procrastination to perfectionism.

I like work; it fascinates me. I can sit and look at it for hours. I love to keep it by me: the idea of getting rid of it nearly breaks my heart.
    Jerome K. Jerome

"Knowledge is power," said Hobbs but "Imagination is more powerful even than knowledge," said Einstein.

I forgot what I was taught. I only remember what I have learned.
    Patrick White

The college graduate is presented with a sheepskin to cover his intellectual nakedness.
    Patrick White

I have never let my schooling interfere with my education.
    Mark Twain

A sign on a high school bulletin board in Dallas read: Free every Monday through Friday - Knowledge, bring your own containers.
    E. C. McKenzie

Education is the period during which you are being instructed by somebody you do not know, about something you do not want to know.
    G. K. Chesterton

Everybody is ignorant, only on different subjects.
    Will Rogers

Education: The path from cocky ignorance to miserable uncertainty.
    Mark Twain

You may send your child to the schoolmaster, but tis the schoolboys who educate him.
    Ralph Waldo Emerson

A native of America who cannot read or write is as rare an appearance as . . . a comet or an earthquake.
    John Adams (1765)

Education is . . . hanging around until you've caught on.
    Robert Frost

If we succeed in giving the love of learning, the learning itself is sure to follow.
    Sir John Lubbock

A problem well stated is a problem half solved.
    Charles F. Kettering

The only place success comes before sweat is in the dictionary - and the road there is often under construction.

Man's mind, once stretched by a new idea, never regains its original dimension.
    Oliver Wendell Holmes

Knowledge comes but wisdom lingers.
    Tennyson

The head learns new things, but the heart forevermore practices old experiences.
    Henry Ward Beecher

No matter how small, we should acknowledge the achievement.

I am always ready to learn, but I do not always like being taught.
    Winston Churchill

Education makes a people easy to lead but difficult to drive; easy to govern but impossible to enslave.
    Lord Brougham

Ah, the insight of hindsight!
    Thurston N. Davis

If people learn from their mistakes, many are getting a fantastic education.

Only hungry minds can become educated.

Responsibility educates.
    Wendell Phillips

You can always spot an educated man. His views are the same as yours.

Not all educated people are intelligent.

The roots of an education are sometimes bitter but the fruits are sweet.

You can get by on charm for about fifteen minutes. After that, you'd better know something.

Education is not received. It is achieved.

Education is a funny thing. At eighteen we knew all the answers - forty years later even the questions confuse us.

The best way to stop kids from seeing R-rated and X-rated movies is to label them "Educational."

Learn from the mistakes made by others. You won't live long enough to make them all yourself.

As an educational device, television rates above everything else. No nation in history has ever known as much as we do about detergents and deodorants.

Education cannot make all of us leaders but it can teach us which leaders to follow.

Among the few things more expensive than an education these days is the lack of it.

I learn by going where I have to go.
    Theodore Roethke

Lack of motivation is often born of lack of achievement.

Some minds are like concrete; thoroughly mixed and permanently set.

If at first you don't succeed, try reading the directions.

In great endeavors, it is glorious even to fail.

It is not what people eat but what they digest, that makes them strong. It is not what they gain but what they save, that makes them rich. It is not what they read but what they remember, that makes them learn.

Opportunities are usually disguised as hard work; so most people don't recognize them.
    Ann Landers

The mind is like a parachute; it functions only when it's open.

The map of progress has no straight road.

There is no limit to how much good you can do it if you don't care who gets the credit.

Reading is to the mind what exercising is to the body.
    Richard Steele

If the going is getting easier, you are not climbing.

Nothing is so fatiguing as the eternal hanging on of an uncompleted task.
    William Games

The gifts of things are never as precious as the gifts of thought.

There is nothing so fatal to character as half-finished tasks.
    David Lloyd George

Skepticism is the highest of duties; blind faith the unpardonable sin.
    Thomas Huxley

Life is like an ice cream cone - you have to learn to lick it.

A person should have enough education so he doesn't have to look up to anyone and enough to be wise enough not to look down.

Thinking is the hardest work there is, which is probably why so few people engage in it.
    Henry Ford

When all other means of communication fail, try words.
    Ashleigh Brilliant

Blessed is the man who expects nothing; he shall never be disappointed.

Investment in knowledge pays the best interest.

To educate a man in mind and not in morals is to educate a menace to society.
    Theodore Roosevelt

Four things to learn in life:
To think clearly without hurry or confusion; To love everybody sincerely; To act in everything with the highest motives; To trust God unhesitatingly.
    Helen Keller

What sculpture is to a block of marble, education is to a human soul.
    Joseph Addison

Oh! this learning, what a thing it is.
    Shakespeare

If we were supposed to talk more than we listen, we would have two mouths and one ear.
    Mark Twain

A ninety-two year old woman said, "I've learned that I still have a lot to learn."

Education makes us what we are.
    C. A. Helvetius

Education, experience and memories are three things no one can take away from you.

If America's only educational duty were to educate everyone who is anxious and willing to learn, we could close down half our schools.
    William F. Buckley Jr.

When things get too easy, it's easy to stop growing.

Old librarians never die, they just check out.

Books are the quietest and most constant of friends; they are the most accessible and wisest of counselors, and the most patient of teachers.
    Charles W. Eliot

The best homework during kindergarten is to surround kids with appropriate books and read to them 365 days a year.
    Allan S. Vann

All that mankind has done, thought, gained, or been; it is lying as in magic preservation in the pages of books.
    Thomas Carlyle

The books which help you most are those which make you think the most.
    Theodore Parker

England has two books, one, which she has made and one which has made her: Shakespeare and the Bible.
    Victor Hugo

Books must be read as deliberately and reservedly as they were written.
    Henry David Thoreau

I cannot live without books.
    Thomas Jefferson

He who can read, but does not, is no better off than one who cannot read.

If a man write a better book, preach a better sermon, or make a better mousetrap than his neighbor, though he build his house in the woods, the world will make a beaten path to his door.
    Ralph Waldo Emerson

A book is like a garden carried in a pocket.
    Chinese Proverb

The worth of a book is to be measured by what you can carry away from it.
    James Bryce

Some books are to be tasted, others to be swallowed, and some few to be chewed and digested: that is, some books are to be read only in parts, others to be read, but not curiously, and some few to be read wholly, and with diligence and attention.
    Francis Bacon

Whoever acknowledges himself to be a zealous follower of truth, of happiness, of wisdom, of science, or even of the faith, must of necessity make himself a lover of books.
    Richard de Bury

Books are divisible into two classes; the books of the hour, and the books of all time.
    John Ruskin

A good title is the title of a successful book.
    Raymond Chandler

When I get a little money, I buy books; and if any is left, I buy food and clothing.
    Desiderius Erasmus

Books are the compasses and telescopes and sextants and charts which other men have prepared to help us navigate the dangerous seas of human life.
    Jesse Lee Bennett

Originality is undetected plagiarism.
    William R. Inge

Take time to read . . . it is the fountain of wisdom.

The love of reading enables a man to exchange the wearisome hours of life, which come to every one, for hours of delight.

No entertainment is so cheap as reading, nor any pleasure so lasting.

The computer is no better than its program.
    Elting E. Morison

Wit is the salt of conversation, not the food.
    William Hazlitt

I don't think necessity is the mother of invention. Invention, in my opinion, arises directly from idleness, possibly also from laziness - to save oneself trouble.
    Agatha Christie

The difference between memorizing information and learning information is understanding.

    You see, but you do not observe. Sir Arthur Conan Doyle

Truth should be the last lesson of the child, and the last aspiration of manhood.
    John Greenleaf Whittier

An ounce of common sense is worth a ton of learning.

If you stop to think, don't forget to get started again.

To find a sanctuary, enter a library.

The less we know the more we suspect.
    H. W. Shaw

The least common of all senses is common sense.

Learning is discovering that something is possible.
    Tehyi Hsieh

It is not good enough to have a good mind; the main thing is to use it well.
    Rene Descartes

Anyone who stops learning is old, whether at twenty or eighty. Anyone who keeps learning stays young. The greatest thing in life is to keep your mind young.
    Henry Ford

The important thing is not so much that every child should be taught, as that every child should be given the wish to learn.
    John Lubbock

It is one thing to show a man that he is in error, and another to put him in possession of truth.
    John Locke

The goal of knowledge is the advancement of knowledge and the dissemination of truth.
    John F. Kennedy

Whoever knocks persistently, gets to enter.

As long as one keeps searching,
the answers come.
    Baez

Language is the dress of thought.
    Samuel Johnson

Our progress as a nation can be no swifter than our progress in education.
    John F. Kennedy

Genius without education is like silver in the mine.
    Benjamin Franklin

Education is a wonderful thing. If you couldn't sign your name, you'd have to pay cash.
    Rita Mae Brown

Education is helping the child realize his potentialities.
    Erich From

A good education should leave much to be desired.
    Alan Gregg

Education is not a product: mark, diploma, job, money - in that order; it is a process, a never-ending one.
    Bel Kaufman

The answer for all our national problems - the answer for all the problems of the world - comes to a single word. That word is "education."
    Lyndon B. Johnson

The object of education is to prepare the young to educate themselves throughout their lives.
    Robert Maynard Hutchins

A sense of accomplishment creates the velocity to excel past complacency.
    Greg Henry Quinn

Respect for the fragility and importance of an individual life is still the first mark of the educated man.
    Norman Cousins

If you educate a man you educate a person, but if you educate a woman you educate a family.
    Ruby Manikan

It is a greater work to educate a child, in the true and larger sense of the word, than to rule a state.
    William Ellery Channing

Facts change too quickly. Only ideas are of importance. We need to help children deal with ideas.
    Beryle Banfield

There is so much of life for, which there is no education and so much of education that has nothing to do with life.
    Dr. Robert L. Geiser

If he is indeed wise, he does not bid you enter the house of his wisdom, but rather leads you to the threshold of your own mind.
    Kahlil Gibran

Education is the best provision for old age.
    Aristotle

Training is everything. The peach was once a bitter almond; cauliflower is nothing but cabbage with a college education.
    Mark Twain

Perhaps the most valuable result of all education is the ability to make yourself do the thing you have to do, when it ought to be done.
    Thomas Henry Hukley

Procrastinating is my sin; it brings me endless sorrow. I really must stop doing it - In fact, I'll start tomorrow.

Education is a means to solving problems, a handmaiden to constructive citizenship, an end in itself, and an object worthy of public support for all of these reasons.
    Thomas Jefferson - 3rd President

It is better to ask some of the questions than to know all the answers.
    James Thurber

As one goes through life, one learns that if you don't paddle your own canoe, you don't move.
    Katharine Hepburn

Take time to think where you are going, or you may not like where you end up.

When someone earns something by virtue of his own effort as opposed to its being given to him, he has infinitely greater appreciation for it.
    Rush Limbaugh

You will never be your best doing it someone else's way; particularly if you utilize talent as opposed to learned skills.

I long to accomplish a great and noble task; but it is my chief duty to accomplish small tasks as if they were great and noble.
    Helen Keller

Make everything as simple as possible, but not simpler.
    Albert Einstein

The dictionary is the only place success comes before work.

The aim of education should be to teach the child to think, not what to think.
    John Dewey

Always remember the distinction between contribution and commitment. Take the matter of bacon and eggs.

The chicken makes a contribution. The pig makes a commitment.
    John Mack Carter

Not only speeches but also conversation can be monopolized, one-sided, insensitive, egocentric, without the courtesy of good listening and sharing.

We learn the rope of life by untying its knots.
    Jean Toomer

The hardest thing in life to learn is which bridge to cross and which to burn.
    David Russell

A good listener is not only popular everywhere, but after a while he knows something.

Many boys are flunking geometry. They just don't know the angles.
    E. C. McKenzie

Failure is success if we learn from it.
    Malcolm S. Forbes

If a man empties his purse into his head, no man can take it from him.
    Benjamin Franklin

Find a way to present knowledge as the antidote for darkness. Strike a match in a dark room.
    Greg Henry Quinn

The greatest friend of Truth is Time, her greatest enemy is Prejudice, and her constant companion is Humility.
    Charles Caleb Colton

All who have meditated on the art of governing mankind are convinced that the fate of empires depends on the education of youth.
    Aristotle

The mind can only absorb what the seat can endure.
    Bud Leftbridge

The greatest undeveloped territory in the world is under your hat.

Knowledge is power!

CRS disease = Can't remember stuff.

Genius, that power which dazzles mortal eyes, is often perseverance in disguise.
    Henry Willard Austin

Ignorance is the night of the mind, a night without moon or star.
    Confucius

The doorstep to the temple of wisdom is knowledge of our own ignorance.
    Charles Haddon Spurgeon

Every man who rises above the common level has received two educations: the first from his teachers; the second, more personal and important, from himself.
    Edward Gibbon

The years teach much, which the days never know.
    Ralph Waldo Emerson

We ought not to look back unless it is to derive useful lessons from past errors and for the purpose of profiting by dear-bought experience.
    George Washington

Only the educated are free.
    Epictetus

Knowledge is the food of the soul. Must they not be utterly unfortunate whose souls are compelled to pass through life always hungering?
    Plato

Man's mind stretched to a new idea never goes back to its original dimensions.
    Oliver Wendell Holmes

A man has only so much knowledge as he puts to work.
    St. Francis of Assisi

The larger the island of knowledge, the longer the shoreline of wonder.
    Ralph W. Sockman

No man really becomes a fool until he stops asking questions.
    Charles P. Steinmetz

As a general rule, the most successful man in life is the man who has the best information.
    Benjamin Disraeli

Common sense in an uncommon degree is what the world calls wisdom.
    Samuel Taylor Coleridge

A fancy education does not a wise man make.

If ignorance is bliss, why aren't more people jumping up and down for joy?

The brightest blaze of intelligence is of less value than the smallest spark of charity.

The error of youth is to believe that intelligence is a substitute for experience, while the error of age is to believe that experience is a substitute for intelligence.

A college graduate is a person who had the chance to get an education.

Tis education forms the common mind; Just as the twig is bent the tree's inclined.
    Alexander Pope

It is the tough situations that provide opportunities to sparkle. Without heat and pressure there would be no diamonds.

There are six mistakes that many of us make: The delusion that individual advancement is made by crushing others down. The tendency to worry about things that cannot be changed or corrected. Insisting that a thing is impossible because we, ourselves, cannot accomplish it. Refusing to set aside trivial preferences in order that important things be accomplished. Neglecting development and refinement. The failure to establish the habit of saving money.

No less than two hours a day should be devoted to exercise.
    Thomas Jefferson

If the man, who wrote the Declaration of Independence, was Secretary of State, and twice the President, could give it two hours a day, we should be able to give it at least 30 minutes.
    John F. Kennedy

Education is necessary for the growth of the mind. In the process of learning, however, we often confuse the ability to perceive what could be with the reality of what is.

I have never met a man so ignorant that I couldn't learn something from him.
    Galileo Galilei

The doctor may learn more about the illness from the way the patient tells the story than from the story itself.
    James B. Herrick

The three foundations of learning: seeing much, suffering much, and studying much.
    Caterall

Four things come not back: the spoken word, the sped arrow, the past life, and the neglected opportunity. The word crisis in Chinese is composed of two characters - one represents danger and the other represents opportunity.
    John F. Kennedy

Four-letter words that changed the world: love, hope, care, heal, work, feel, duty, home, good, kind, pity, rest, seek, pray, live.

It is astonishing what power words have over man.
    Napoleon Bonaparte

Better one word before than two after.

For good or ill, your conversation is your advertisement. Every time you open your mouth you let men look into your mind.
    Bruce Barton

The value of the average conversation could be enormously improved by the constant use of four simple words: "I do not know."
    Andre Maurois

A single conversation with a wise man is better than ten years of study.

A word from the heart goes straight to the heart.
    Abbe Huvelin

One of the reasons why so few people are to be found who seem sensible and pleasant in conversation is that almost everybody is thinking about what he wants to say himself, rather than about answering clearly what is being said to him. One secret of successful conversation is learning to disagree without being disagreeable. It isn't what but how you speak that makes all the difference. Ben Franklin used to remark diplomatically, "On this point, I agree.
But on the other, if you don't mind, may I take exception."
    Jack Harrison Pollack

All words are pegs to hang ideas on.
    Henry Ward Beecher

Words are a powerful drug, and many men are destroyed from their much use.
    R. E. Phillips

Habit, if not resisted, soon becomes necessity.
    St. Augustine

The mind unlearns with difficulty what it has long learned.
    Seneca

If I look confused it's because I'm thinking.
    Sam Goldwyn

People will listen a great deal more patiently while you explain your mistakes than when you explain your successes.
    Wilbur N. Nesbit

One cardinal rule: One must always listen to the patient.
    Dr. Oliver

The larger the number of people involved in any given decision, the greater the pressure for conformity.

Common sense is the knack of seeing things as they are, and doing things as they ought to be done.

Nothing astonishes men so much as common sense and plain dealing.
    Ralph Waldo Emerson

Half of the world's problems are caused by poor communications. The other half are caused by good communications.

There is no expedient to which a man will not go to avoid the real labor of thinking.
    Thomas A. Edison

The probable reason some people get lost in thought is because it is unfamiliar territory to them.

Nothing in the world can take the place of persistence. Talent will not; nothing is more common than unsuccessful men with talent. Genius will not; unrewarded genius is almost a proverb. Education will not; the world is full of educated derelicts. Persistence and determination alone are omnipotent.

The slogan "press on!" has solved and always will solve the problems of the human race.
　　Calvin Coolidge

I believe that every right implies a responsibility; every opportunity, an obligation; every possession, duty.
　　John D. Rockefeller, Jr.

Our main business is not to see what lies dimly at a distance, but to do what lies clearly at hand.
　　Thomas Carlyle

Make it a point to do something every day that you don't want to do. This is the golden rule for acquiring the habit of doing your duty without pain.
　　Mark Twain

Knowledge of your duties is the most essential part of the philosophy of life. If you avoid duty, you avoid action. The world demands results.
　　George W. Goethals

There are obviously two educations: One should teach us how to make a living. The other should teach us how to live.
　　James Truslow Adams

Universities are full of knowledge; the freshmen bring a little in and the seniors take none away, and knowledge accumulates.
　　Abbott Lowell

Strange how much you've got to know before you know how little you know.

Those who think they know it all are very annoying to those of us who do.
　　Robert K. Mueller

The trouble with the world is not that people know too little, but that they know so many things that ain't so.
　　Mark Twain

Education is what's left over when you subtract what you've forgotten from what you've learned.

. . . Education is a progressive discovery of our own ignorance.
　　Will Durant

The purpose of education is to provide everyone with the opportunity to learn how best he may serve the world.

Economists report that a college education adds many thousands of dollars to a man's lifetime income - which he then spends sending his son to college.
　　Bill Vaughan

Creative minds always have been known to survive any kind of bad training.
　　Anna Freud Thinking is hard work.

Creativity is inventing, experimenting, growing, taking risks, breaking rules, making mistakes, and having fun.
　　Mary Lou Cook

One worthwhile task carried to a successful conclusion is worth half a hundred half-finished tasks.
　　B. C. Forbes

Our species is the only creative species, and it has only one creative instrument, the individual mind and spirit of a man. Nothing was ever created by two men. There are no good collaborations, whether in music, in art, in poetry, in mathematics, in philosophy. Once the miracle of creation has taken place, the group can build and extend it, but the group never invents anything. The

preciousness lies in the lonely mind of a man.
    John Steinbeck

Teamwork may be good for morale, but when new ideas are needed, it's best to let people work on their own. Research shows that people who were left by themselves to think about subjects they considered relevant came up with three times as many ideas as those who brainstormed in groups. Researchers believe that when people work in groups, their creativity is inhibited by fear of criticism and real or perceived pressures to conform.

The greatest of the arts is the art of living together.
    William Lyon Phelps

A man that has a taste of music, painting, or architecture, is like one that has another sense, when compared with such as have no relish of those arts.
Joseph Addison

The dramatist, like the poet, is born, not made.
    William Winter

Of all imitators, dramatists are the most perverse, the most unconscionable, or the most unconscious, and have been so time out of mind.
    Edgar Allen Poe

The most difficult character in comedy is that of the fool, and he must be no simpleton that plays that part.
    Miguel de Cervantes

Music is a revelation; a revelation loftier than all wisdom and all philosophy.
    Ludwig van Beethoven

There's music in the sighing of a reed;
There's music in the gushing of a rill;
There's music in all things, if we have ears;
the earth is but the music of the spheres.
    George Gordon, Lord Byron

Where words fail, music speaks.
    Hans Christian Andersen

We love music for the buried hopes, the garnered memories, and the tender feelings it can summon at a touch.
    Samuel Rogers

Music is love in search of a word.
    Sidney Lanier

People of all generations react to my music (singing) in the same way. They listen, they clap their hands, they tap their feet, they sing along, sometimes they cry, sometimes they smile, but most often they feel uplifted . . . they have a good time.
    John Denver

Such sweet compulsion doth in music lie.
    John Milton

Architecture is frozen music.
    Johann Wolfgang von Goethe

Without music, life would be a mistake.
    Friedrich Nietzsche

Music hath charms to soothe the savage beast.
    James Bramston

No entertainment is so cheap as reading, nor any pleasure so lasting.

The love of reading enables a man to exchange the wearisome hours of life, which come to every one, for hours of delight.

It's an odd idea for someone like me to keep a diary; not only because I have never done so before, but because it seems to me that neither I - nor for that matter anyone else - will be interested in the unbosoming of a thirteen-year-old schoolgirl. Still, what does that matter? I want to write, but more than that, I want to bring out all kinds of things that lie buried deep in my heart.
    Anne Frank, The Diary of a Young Girl

I write to find out what I am thinking about.
    Edward Albee

Nothing great was ever achieved without enthusiasm. It overcomes discouragement and gets things done. It is the magic quality. And the remarkable thing is - it's contagious!

Copyright means copy it right out of the book.

Words are things; and a small drop of ink, falling like dew upon a thought, produces that which makes thousands, perhaps millions, think.
    Lord Byron

The difference between the right word and the almost right word is the difference between lightning and the lightning bug.
    Mark Twain

    The pen is mightier than the sword.
    Bulwer - Lytton

Writing is the hardest way of earning a living, with the possible exception of wrestling alligators.
    Olin Miller

Writing a book is an adventure. To begin with, it is a toy and an amusement. Then it becomes a mistress, then it becomes a master, and then it becomes a tyrant. The last phase is that just as you are about to be reconciled to your servitude, you kill the monster, and fling him to the public.
    Winston Churchill

Write freely and as rapidly as possible and throw the whole thing on paper.
Never correct or rewrite until the whole thing is down. Rewrite in process is usually found to be an excuse for not going on.
    John Steinbeck

The computer is not a toy it is a tool.

I write the ending first. Nobody reads a book to get to the middle.
    Mickey Spillane

The greatest part of a writer's time is spent in reading, in order to write; a man will turn over a half a library to make one book.
    Samuel Johnson

Doctors bury their mistakes. Lawyers hang theirs. And journalists put theirs on the front page.

The last thing we decide in writing a book is what to put first.
    Blaise Pascal

Curiosity is one of the permanent and certain characteristics of a vigorous intellect.
    Samuel Johnson

I disapprove of what you say, but I will defend to the death, your right to say it.
    Voltaire

I have yet to see a piece of writing, political or non-political, that doesn't have a slant. All writing slants the way a writer leans, and no man is born perpendicular, although many men are born upright. The beauty of the American free press is that the slants and the twists and the distortions come from so

many directions, and the special interests are so numerous, the reader must sift and sort and check and countercheck in order to find out what the score is.
    E. B. White

Never talk about what you are going to do until after you have written it.
    Mario Puzo

It helps to read the sentence aloud.
    Harry Kemelman

Don't tell anybody what your book is about and don't show it until it's finished. It's not that anybody will steal your idea but that all the energy that goes into the writing of your story will be dissipated.
    David Wallechinsky

You can never know enough about your characters.
    W. Somerset Maugham

Your audience is one single reader. I have found that sometimes it helps to pick out one person - a real person you know - or an imagined person and write to that one.
    John Steinbeck

He whose heart has been set on the love of learning and true wisdom, and has exercised this part of himself, that man must without fail have thoughts that are immortal and divine, if he lay hold on truth.
    Plato

Learning is acquired by reading books; but the much more necessary learning, the knowledge of the world, is only to be acquired by reading men, and studying all the various editions of them.
    Lord Chesterfield

Genius borrows nobly.
    Emerson

There's nothing new under the sun, we borrow and adapt constantly.

All authors draw on what has been written before.

Transformation is the essence of the authorship process.

Studying is a lifelong proposition.

Failure at the first try, need not spell the end of the road or the shattering of a dream.

If you have trubble spelling wurds, look in the dickshunary.

It is not only the I.Q. but the "I will" which is important in education.

If you don't understand it, oppose it!

The only thing more expensive than education is ignorance.

When everyone thinks alike, few are doing much thinking.

Poverty and shame shall be to him that refuseth instruction.
    Proverbs 13:18

Caution: Be sure brain is engaged before putting mouth in gear.

Only failure can be accomplished without effort.

Indeed, one of the ultimate advantages of education is simply coming to an end of it.
    B. F. Skinner

Chapter 3

SCHOOL IS ALWAYS IN SESSION AND LIFE CHALLENGES US TO EXCEL AT BEING BOTH ENTHUSIASTIC STUDENTS AND INSPIRED TEACHERS.
H.J. B.

Adult education is something that will continue as long as kids have homework.

Kindness is contagious.

You can catch more flies with honey than with vinegar.

You may have tangible wealth untold;
Caskets of jewels and coffers of gold,
Richer than I you can never be -
I had a Mother who read to me.
    Strickland Gillilan

One father is more than a hundred school-masters.
    George Herbert

A mother's heart is the child's schoolroom.
    Henry Ward Beecher

There must be such a thing as a child with average ability, but you can't find a parent who will admit that it is his child.
    Thomas Bailey

School teachers are not fully appreciated by parents until it rains all day Saturday and Sunday.

A student's success in school starts in the heads and hearts of his or her parents and teachers. The way we see them, the way they see themselves, is what they will become.
    Linda Holt

One of the hardest facts of life to learn for young people is that one-day they will be as stupid as their parents.

The biggest room in the world is the room for improvement.

It is easier to keep up than to catch up.

Schools are where we learn to think and dream. They shape the future for each new generation of Americans . . . and are the bedrock of our success as a nation.

Sometimes, one day in school can make the difference for a lifetime: The day you learn how to read. The day you win an award in the science fair. The day you start thinking, "I can" instead of "I can't."

Conscience is the compass; self- discipline the rudder. Make choices based on moral and honorable convictions, and you will be the master of your own ship.
    Greg Henry Quinn

This is a non-profit school. We didn't plan it that way, but that's how it happened.

Days are like suitcases - all the same size, but some people pack more into them.

The schools of the country are its future in miniature.
    Tehyi Hsieh

. . . In the schoolhouse we have the heart of the whole society.
    Henry Golden

A sign over the country school read: "We guarantee satisfaction or you will get your child back."

As the sun makes ice melt, kindness causes misunderstanding, mistrust, and hostility to evaporate.
    Albert Schweitzer

School is always in session and life challenges us to excel at being both enthusiastic students and inspired teachers.
    H. J. Brown

When someone gives you a free ticket, don't complain about the show.

Well-arranged time is the surest mark of a well-arranged mind.

Don't hurry, don't worry,
Do your best, and leave the rest.

The quitter never wins. The winner never quits.

People do not lack strength, they lack will.

A special note for Mom from the kindergarten teacher:
"If you promise not to believe everything your child says happens at school, I'll promise not to believe everything he says happens at home."
    Harry B. Otis

He, who cannot obey, cannot command.
    Benjamin Franklin

Before I judge my neighbor, let me walk a mile in his moccasins.

Kind words are like honey - enjoyable and healthful.
    The Bible

Be not afraid of growing slowly; be afraid only of standing still.

If you need a helping hand you'll find one at the end of your arm.

The Supreme Court has handed down the Eleventh Commandment: "Thou shalt not, in thy classroom, read the first ten."
    Fletcher Knebel

Since thou art not sure of a minute, throw not away an hour.
    Benjamin Franklin

A person who always watches the clock will never become the man of the hour.

We never shall have any more time. We have, and we have always had, all the time there is.
    Arnold Bennett

Never apologize for showing feelings. Remember that when you do, you apologize for the truth.
    Benjamin Disraeli

He who has learned how to laugh at himself shall never cease to be entertained.
    John Powell

Every survival kit should include a sense of humor.

A person without a sense of humor is like a wagon without springs - jolted by every pebble in the road.
    Henry Ward Beecher

We are all alike, on the inside.
    Mark Twain

The deepest principle in human nature is the craving to be appreciated.
    William James

Birds of a feather will flock together.
    Minsheu

As schools flourish, the community flourishes.

It is hard to convince a high-school student that he will encounter a lot of problems more difficult than those of algebra and geometry.
    Edgar W. Howe

A child miseducated is a child lost.
    John F. Kennedy

The pupil, who is never required to do what he cannot do, never does what he can do.
    John Stuart Mill

We cannot always build the future for our youth, but we can build our youth for the future.
    Franklin D. Roosevelt

Dignity is an extraordinarily important word and I meet few adults in my life who have much sense of a child's dignity or need for it.
    John Holt

No tests that I know of measure important human qualities such as motivation, caring, sensitivity, perseverance, and integrity. They certainly do not measure personal worth the kind of human being a person is or will be.
    Gregory Anrig

Students can learn anything they put their minds to, their hearts in, and their hands on.

One thing stopped me from going to college, high school.
    Henny Youngman

A child can ask many questions the wisest man cannot answer.

No child is good at everything, but every child is good at something.
    Arlene Uslander

You have no idea how good you can be at whatever you want to do. You don't know because you are trapped in situations where you either can't or are afraid to be yourself.

It is never safe to consider individuals in groups, classes, or races. To ascribe virtues or vices to all the individuals of a group is as senseless as it is unjust and inaccurate.

Gossip is putting two and two together and making five.

I still remember my college days - all four of them.
    Henny Youngman

How many friends would remain if all persons knew what each said of the other?

Friends can be made by many acts but can be lost by one.

When we do the best we can, we never know what miracle is wrought in our own life, or in the life of another.
    Helen Keller

I ask but this, that whenever a thing is right it take no courage to do it, that whenever a thing be wrong, it may have no power of temptation over me.

Failure only comes when you give up, for failure is simply a return to the starting point knowing more than you did when you started.

I am a work in progress.

Whatever is worth doing at all, is worth doing well.
    Lord Chesterfield

Be the labor great or small Do it well or not at all.

You can make more friends in two months by becoming interested in other people than you can in two years by trying to get other people interested in you.
    Dale Carnegie

Who is your best friend? It is he or she who helps you bring out of yourself the best that is in you.
    Henry Ford

One day at a time; we learn this lesson with difficulty but it holds the key to life and peace.

An admission of error is a sign of strength rather than a weakness.

Believe in yourself. Keep your sense of humor.

Life does not always feel good.

Today, our youth face a serious problem; they believe they are always supposed to feel good, and have instant gratification.

We have become a generation of instant and fast everything.

People, who live in glass houses, should never throw stones.

Those who complain about the way the ball bounces, are usually the ones who dropped it in the first place.

Do it tomorrow. You've made enough mistakes today.

If at first you succeed, try not to look shocked.

If at first you don't succeed, you're running about average.

The toughest thing about homework is getting mom and pop to agree on the same answer.
    Joey Adams

The kids in my old neighborhood never drop out of school. There'd be nobody to drive the teachers crazy.
    Milton Berle

Children are our most valuable natural resource.
    Herbert Hoover

Be satisfied with nothing but your best.
    Edward Rowland Sill

Ability will enable a person to get to the top, but it takes character to keep him there.

In matters of style, swim with the current; in matters of principle, stand like a rock.
    Thomas Jefferson

Don't be content with being average. Average is as close to the bottom as it is to the top.

Successful people try, practice, and wander down blind alleys. They pay their dues but they don't give up.

Always speak the truth and you'll never be concerned with your memory.

Be cheerful! Of all the things you wear, your expression is the most important.

Smile, it increases your face value.

Don't be afraid to ask dumb questions. They're easier to handle than dumb mistakes.

The great calamity is not to have failed but to have failed to try.

He is only exempt from failures who makes no efforts.

Learn the skills you need and keep pushing yourself.

You shouldn't compare yourself to the best others can do, but to the best that you can do.

The more creative you are, the more things you notice.

You should never be too busy to say "please" and "thank you."

Untold treasures are found in the imagination of a child.

If I'm in trouble at school, I'm in more trouble at home.

A person's degree of self-confidence greatly determines his success.

Generous people seldom have emotional and mental problems.

If you are all wrapped up in yourself, you are overdressed.
    Halverson

The young people of today are the leaders of tomorrow, but we sometimes wonder whether they are going to be followed or chased.

If all the year were playing . . . to sport, would be as tedious as to work.
    William Shakespeare

Children require guidance and sympathy far more than instruction.
    Anne Sullivan

There is a fountain of youth; it is your mind, your talents, and the creativity you bring to your life.
    Loren

In youth we learn; in age we understand.
    Von Ebner-Eschenbach

When one helps another, both are strong.
    German Proverb

You can never have too many friends.

Many people give up just when they are about to achieve success.

Self-pity is a waste of time.

We grow when we push ourselves beyond what we already know.

Respect every viewpoint. No two people can stand in the exact same place at the exact same time.
    Greg Henry Quinn

The least creative child is the one most fearful of failure.

When our society looks at us and says our schools are troubled, what they are really saying is that our society is troubled and by implication they are saying, "Help us, dear teachers. You are our hope."
    Linda Holt

There's never a snow day on the day I have a big test.

To see yourself in a different light, look through someone else's eyes.

Imagination is the embryo of the future. Imagination is at its peak in children.

Mourn not your mistakes; rather mourn the lost opportunities to correct them.

Failure like success, is the result of an attempt.

Every single human being is of infinite worth and value - especially kids.
    Billy Dean Nave Jr.

Good manners and soft words have brought many a difficult thing to pass.
    Aesop

Politeness is like an air cushion; there may be nothing in it, but it eases our jolts wonderfully.
    Will Carleton

The greater the man, the greater the courtesy.
    Alfred Lord Tennyson

The most skillful flattery is to let a person talk on, and be a listener.
    Joseph Addison

An idle brain is the devil's workshop.

A day of accomplishment is a good day.

Invest in children. A child's life will be rich only if there are more deposits than withdrawals.
    Greg Henry Quinn

Personality is the clothing; character is the soul.

Life is not so short but there is always time enough for courtesy.
    Ralph Waldo Emerson

Everything is funny as long as it is happening to somebody else.
    Will Rogers

All's well that ends well.
    Shakespeare

Children are like wet cement, whatever falls on them, leaves an impression.
    Bob Kittell

Two roads diverged in a wood, and I - I took the one less traveled by, and that has made all the difference.
    Robert Frost

That's one small step for a man, one giant leap for mankind.
    Neil Armstrong, 1969

Children are not things to be molded but people to be unfolded.
    Bob Kittell

What do we live for if not to make life less difficult for those that follow?
    Mark Twain

Let's resolve to do the best we can with what we've got.
    William Feather

Truth is the most valuable thing we have. Let us economize it.
    Mark Twain

To escape criticism - do nothing, say nothing, be nothing.
    Elbert Hubbard

Conceit is a queer disease; it makes everybody sick but the one who has it.

Never let the fear of striking out get in your way.
    George Herman (Babe) Ruth

Twelve Things to Remember:
The value of time
The success of perseverance
The pleasure of working
The dignity of simplicity
The worth of character
The power of kindness
The influence of example
The obligation of duty
The wisdom of economy
The virtue of patience
The improvement of talent
The joy of origination
    Marshall Field

Honesty is the first chapter of the book of wisdom.
    Thomas Jefferson

Two wrongs - don't make a right!

A good reputation is a person's greatest asset.

The only exercise some people get is jumping to conclusions, running down their friends, sidestepping responsibility, dodging issues, passing the buck, and pushing their luck.

Prolonged idleness paralyzes initiative.

If your life is free of failures, you're probably not taking enough risks.

A person's posture says a lot about his or her self-confidence.

Attractiveness is a positive caring attitude and has nothing to do with face-lifts or nose jobs.

It is easier to fight for one's principles than it is to live up to them.

My teacher always calls on me the one time I don't know the answer.

Win without boasting. Lose without excuse.
    Albert Payson Terhune

Associate with men of good quality, if you esteem your own reputation; for it is better to be alone than in bad company.
    George Washington

Tell me thy company and I will tell thee what thou art.
    Cervantes

The best index to a person's character is how he treats people who can't do him any good, and how he treats people who can't fight back.
    Abigail Van Buren

When the character of a man is not clear to you, look at his friends.

The late blooming virtues can be the very best.

Sometimes a person's mind is stretched by a new idea and never does go back to its old dimensions.
    Oliver Wendell Holmes

If nobody dropped out at the eight grade, who would hire the college graduates?

Ideas are like children - no matter how much you admire someone else's you can't help liking your own best.

Laziness grows on people; it begins in cobwebs and ends in iron chains.
    M. Hale

Laziness travels so slowly that poverty soon overtakes him.

To err is human, but when the eraser wears out ahead of the pencil, you're overdoing it.
    J. Jenkins

Human action can be modified to some extent, but human nature cannot be changed.
    Abraham Lincoln
    Don't cry over spilt milk.

It is when we forget ourselves that we do things that are most likely to be remembered.

In the long run, the pessimist may be proved right, but the optimist has a better time on the trip.

Some people are always grumbling because roses have thorns; I am thankful that thorns have roses.
    Alphonse Karr

There are two kinds of people in the world: Those who come into a room and say, "Here I am!" and those who come in and say, "Ah, there you are!"

The iron rule: Don't do for others what they wouldn't take the trouble to do for themselves.
    D. Fulton

He that would jest must take a jest; else to let it alone were best.

Many a true word is spoke in jest.
Be humble or you'll stumble.
    Dwight L. Moody

Don't cross that bridge until you come to it.

A man's real worth is determined by what he does when he has nothing to do.

The reason why worry kills more than work is that more people worry than work.
    Robert Frost

To win you have to risk loss.
    Jean Claude Killy

A little spark of accomplishment can ignite great endeavors.

Together we can help each other achieve great things.

The value of a man's advice is the way he applies it to himself.
    Barry Cornwall

Criticism is dangerous, because it wounds a man's precious pride, hurts his sense of importance and arouses his resentment.
    Dale Carnegie

A California survey indicates that the more a student watches television, the worse he does in school. California Schools Superintendent Wilson Riles said that no matter how much homework the students did, how intelligent they were or how much money their parents made, the relationship between TV and test scores was practically identical.
    The Associated Press, October 1980

TV may be a training course in the art of inattention.

Yale University's Family Television Research Center states that TV viewing stunts the growth of imagination in the crucial ages between three and five.
Such children make up fewer games and imaginary playmates.

Try going a week without television. You will probably sense some withdrawal pains.

American children witness between 11,000 and 13,000 acts of violence on TV by the age of fifteen.

As children are exposed to television with its messages of sex and violence, they expose themselves to those ideals and their actions will be affected.

As a man thinketh in his heart so is he.
    The Bible

Try not to become a man of success, but rather become a man of value.
    Albert Einstein

All that is necessary for evil to triumph is for good men to do nothing.

You've got to get up to bat first.

You'll miss 100% of the shots you never take.

Alcohol is used by a majority of the adult population and creates more problems than all other drugs combined.
    Robert Elliott

There is a deep tendency in human nature to become what we imagine ourselves to be.
    William Ernest Hocking

One, who fears, limits his activities. Failure is only the opportunity to more intelligently begin again.
    Henry Ford

One of the rarest things that man ever does is to do the best he can.
    Josh Billings

If I had influence with the good fairy who is supposed to preside over the christening of all children I should ask that her gift to each child be a sense of wonder so indestructible that it would last throughout life, and unfailing antidote against the boredom and disenchantment of later years, the sterile preoccupation with things that are artificial, the alienation from the sources of our strength.
    Rachel Carson

A sound discretion is not so much indicated by never making a mistake, as by never repeating it.
    Christian Bovee

It is not worth while to go round the world to count the cats in Zanzibar.
    Henry David Thoreau

Too many parents are out airing their views when they should be home viewing their heirs.

For nations in history, just as for individuals in everyday life, character determines destiny . . . The future of our nation will be determined more than anything else by the character of our children.
    Ronald Wilson Reagan

The lack of confidence to excel often leads to the acceptance of merely passing.

Think little of what others think of you. Work enjoyed is as much fun as leisure.

When all else fails, read the instructions.

It's better to keep your mouth shut and appear stupid than to open it and remove all doubt.
    Mark Twain

Thinking is the hardest work there is, which is the probable reason why so few engage in it.
    Henry Ford

Every human being is intended to have a character of his own; to be what no other is, and to do what no other can do.
    William Ellery Channing

Every man has written himself a continent of undiscovered character. Happy is he who proves the Columbus of his soul.
    Johann Wolfgang von Goethe

For every ailment under the sun, There is a remedy, or there is none; If there be one, try to find it; If there be none, never mind it.
    Mother Goose

Thirteen Rules for Good Behavior:
1. Don't eat or drink too much.
2. Don't joke or talk too much.
3. Keep your things neat.
4. Do whatever you set out to do.
5. Don't spend too much money.
6. Don't waste time.
7. Be sincere.
8. Be fair.
9. Don't go to extremes.
10. Keep neat and clean.
11. Keep calm.
12. Don't mess with girls.
13. Don't show off.
    Benjamin Franklin

Climbing the rungs of an effort ladder to successful attitudes:
1. I won't.
2. I can't.
3. I don't know how.
4. I'll think about it.
5. I wish I could.
6. I think I might.
7. I might.
8. I think I can.
9. I can.
10. I will.
11. Nothing will stop me.
12. I did it.
13. I did even more than was expected.

A well-developed sense of humor is the pole that adds balance to your steps as you walk the tightrope of life.
    William A. Ward

If you could choose one characteristic that would get you through life, choose a sense of humor.
    Jennifer Jones

Keep away from people who try to belittle your ambitions. Small people always do that, but the really great make you feel that you, too, can become great.
    Mark Twain

A dreamer lives forever.

You can't help a man uphill without getting closer to the top yourself.

Down in their hearts, wise men know this truth: The only way to help yourself is to help others.
    Elbert Hubbard

Sometimes nothing gives you a helping hand like receiving a kick in the pants.

An egotist is not a man who thinks too much of himself. He is a man who thinks too little of other people.
    J. F. Newton

Make new friends, but keep the old, one is silver but the other is gold.

He who seeks a friend without a fault, will remain without one.

True friendship is like sound health, the value of it is seldom known until it is lost.

There are three kinds of friends: best friends, guest friends, and pest friends.

When you throw mud at someone, you are the one who is losing ground.

Nobody can make you feel inferior without your consent.
    Eleanor Roosevelt

People are lonely because they build walls instead of bridges.

One's richest treasure is that of a loyal friend.

There is no right way to do the wrong thing.

He who sows courtesy reaps friendship, and he who plants kindness gathers love.

A friend is a present you give yourself.
    Robert Louis Stevenson

Many will seek your friendship while you have much to give. When you need to receive the number of your friends will be diminished, but their quality will be improved.

May we never have friends who, like shadows, keep close to us in the sunshine, only to desert us on a cloudy day.

He, who does not thank for little, will not thank for much.
    Estonian Proverb

Real friends are those who when you've made a fool of yourself, don't feel that you've done a permanent job.

A person all wrapped up in himself makes a very small package.

You are young only once, but you can stay immature for life.

Laughter is a tranquilizer with no side effects.
    Arnold Glasow

If you laugh at your troubles you will never run out of something to laugh about.

The real character of a man may be measured by what he does when no one is looking.

Silence is golden.

Talent may develop in solitude, but character is developed in society.

Children may close their ears to advice, but they open their eyes to example.

Character and ideals are catching. When you associate with men who aspire to the highest and the best, you expose yourself to the qualities that make men great.

If at first you don't succeed, you'll get a lot of advice.

Participation increases gain.

The amount of pain we inflict upon others is directly proportional to the amount we feel within us.

A smile is the gentle curved line that sets a lot of things straight.

The smallest good deed is better than the grandest good intention.

Fools names and fools faces always appear in public places.

Don't break the silence unless you can improve on it.

Children are the only people wise enough to enjoy today without regretting yesterday or fearing tomorrow.

As long as there are pupils there will be parents to contend with. All types of parents: kind, understanding parents; unreasonable parents; quick-tempered parents; and blind-to-the-faults-of-their- offspring parents.

A child's dream: no teachers, no schools.

Opportunity knocks only once. Temptation kicks the door in.

Children require guidance and sympathy far more than instruction.
    Anne Sullivan

True friendship comes when silence between two people is comfortable.

The school of ignorance is the most expensive school.

"You know" are words used by students who don't.

Few things are as embarrassing as watching someone else do what you said couldn't be done.

What is morality? It is what makes you feel good after.
    Ernest Hemingway

Tomorrow is not promised to us, so take today and make the most of it.

I am much afraid that schools will prove to be great gates of hell, unless they diligently labor in explaining the Holy Scriptures, engraving them in the hearts of youth, I advise no one to place his child where the Scriptures do not reign paramount, every institution in which men are not increasingly occupied with the word of God must become corrupt.
    Martin Luther

Happiness is found along the way, not at the end of the road.
    UpDegraff

Students are like tacks: if they have good heads and are pointed in the right direction, they serve their purpose well.

Some students seem to fall for everything and stand for nothing.

Children, like canoes, are more easily controlled if paddled from the rear.

Nature gives us two ears, two eyes, and but one tongue, so that we should hear and see more than we speak.

Anyone who thinks by the inch and talks by the yard should be moved by the foot.

After all is said and done, more is usually said than done.

A slip of the foot you may soon recover, but a slip of the tongue you may never get over.

A gossip is the top man on a quote 'em pole.

Don't talk about yourself. Others will take care of that when you leave.

The light bulb was Thomas Edison's bright idea. What's yours?

Many students these days need a kick in the seat of their can'ts.

The student who fails to plan, plans to fail.

If you think you're a wit, make sure you're not half right.

Before beginning a project, plan ahead.

Too many students today are temper-mental - 90% temper and 10% mental.

Triumph is just umph added to try. It's time to knock the "t" off of "can't."

If you are not afraid to face the music, you may some day lead the band.

Fill your life with experiences not excuses.

Life is not a plateau to be reached, but a river to be sailed.

A smooth sea never made a skillful mariner.

The man who rows the boat doesn't have time to rock it.

We cannot direct the wind, but we can adjust our sails.

It is better to be alone than in bad company.

Yard by yard
   Life is hard.
Inch by inch,
   It's a cinch.

Luck is another name for hard work.

A hero is an ordinary man who is brave a little longer.

The reward of a thing well done is to have done it.

Chapter 4

**ONE OF THE TESTS OF LEADERSHIP IS THE
ABILITY TO RECOGNIZE A PROBLEM BEFORE
IT BECOMES AN EMERGENCY.
ARNOLD H. GLASOW**

The ability to accept responsibility is the measure of a man.
    Roy L. Smith

The trouble with being punctual is that nobody is there to appreciate it.
    Franklin P. Jones

The only person worse than a quitter, is the one who cannot bring himself to begin.

Some people are like tea bags. They don't know their own strength until they get into hot water.
    Herb True

Trouble is usually produced by those who produce nothing else.

The only way to get the best of an argument is to avoid it.
    Dale Carnegie

Do not do for children what they can do for themselves.

It's surprising how often a narrow mind and a wide mouth go together.

Color is beautiful; so are understanding and acceptance.

Classroom control is like controlling a fire. If you catch it early, it is easy to handle.

Teamwork is essential - it allows the blame to be shared.

The worst behaved child in the classroom always has the best attendance record.

Discipline is finding effective alternatives to punishment.
    Dr. Haim Ginott

It's important for the child to trust the person who enforces the discipline. The child needs to feel that the person setting the limits is really concerned about him.
    Dr. Lee Salk

Staying calm is the best way to take the wind out of an angry person's sails.

Pick battles big enough to matter, small enough to win.
    Jonathan Kozol

Find out where your enemy is. Get him as soon as you can. Strike at him as hard as you can and as often as you can, and keep moving on.
    Ulysses S. Grant

Fire is the test of gold, adversity of strong men.
    Seneca

Patience is bitter, but its fruit is sweet.

Make the most of the best and the least of the worst.

It's a rough road that leads to greatness. \
    Seneca

Give a little love to a child and you get a great deal back.
    John Ruskin

He surely is most in need of another's patience, who has none of his own.

Correction does much, but encouragement does more. Encouragement after censure is as the sun after a shower.
    Johann Wolfgang von Goethe

Thirteen Excuses:
The list below is the current popularity rating for excuses. To save time for both of us, please give your excuse by number.
1. I thought I told you.
2. That's the way we've always done it.
3. No one told me to go ahead.
4. I didn't think it was very important.
5. I'm so busy I just can't get around to it.
6. Why bother? The admiral won't buy it.
7. I didn't know you were in a hurry for it.
8. That's his job, not mine.
9. I forgot.
10. I'm waiting for an OK.
11. That's not in my department.
12. How did I know this was different?
13. Wait till the boss comes back and ask him.

Consider wherein you agree with your opponent rather than wherein you differ.

He who has not forgiven an enemy has never yet tasted one of the most sublime enjoyments of life.

Charity - the one thing we can give away without losing it.
    Horace Smith

We have committed the Golden Rule to memory; let us now commit it to life.
    Edwin Markham

The ally of tolerance is knowledge. The understanding of another's nature precludes hostility.

Diplomacy is to do and say the nastiest thing in the nicest way.

Your actions are so loud; I can't hear what you are saying.

One of the marks of a mature person is the ability to dissent without creating dissension.
    Don Robinson

Habits are at first cobwebs, then cables.
    Spanish Proverb

At doing what we shouldn't, we are all experts.

Always remember that what happens around us is largely outside our control, but the way we choose to react to it is inside our control.

An ounce of prevention is worth a pound of cure.

Our words may hide our thoughts, but our actions will reveal them.

Patting a student on the back is the best way to get a chip off his shoulder.

No matter how thin you slice it, there are always two sides.

It doesn't cost anything to be nice.

Do not use a hatchet to remove a fly from your friend's forehead.
    Chinese Proverb

Time and words cannot be recalled.

It is easier to pull down than to build up.

What you don't see with your eyes, don't invent with your mouth.

It is a badge of honor to accept valid criticism.
     The Bible

Love is like the five loaves and two fishes. It doesn't start to multiply until you give it away.

Good order is the foundation of all good things.
     Edmund Burke

Reprove a friend in secret, but praise him before others.
     Leonardo da Vinci

Discipline is the rudimentary thread of the learning cloak.

Panic exists in an uncontrollable environment. Uncontrollable environments are those that were not anticipated.

Use the four-step plan in every event; anticipate, plan, control, relax.

The trouble with trouble is that it starts out as fun.

Denial is a problem's nourishment. Confrontation is its demise.

Tact is the ability to close your mouth before someone else wants to.

The die is cast. Julius Caesar

The best way out of difficulty is through it.

Once the facts are clear, the decisions jump out at you.
     Peter Drucker

Oh, what a wicked web we weave, when we practice to deceive.

A wise man restrains his anger and overlooks insults.
     The Bible

Keep out of ruts; a rut is something, which if traveled in too much, becomes a ditch.
     Arthur Guiterman

Error is the discipline through which we advance.
     William Channing

An error gracefully acknowledged is a victory won.
     Caroline L. Gascoigne

The best way to destroy your enemy is to make him your friend.
     Abraham Lincoln

Compassion and discipline are a compatible paradox.

The most successful government has the fewest police. Order depends on self-discipline.

Humiliation is the cleanser that removes the ego to reveal the fool.

Do not anticipate trouble or worry about what may never happen.
     Benjamin Franklin

Nobody likes having salt rubbed into his or her wounds, even if it is the salt of the earth.
     Rebecca West

The art of being wise is the art of knowing what to overlook.
    William James

A man should never be ashamed to say he has been wrong, which is to say, in other words that he is wiser today than he was yesterday.
    Alexander Pope

Nothing very bad or very good ever lasts very long.

You should never fight a battle if there is nothing to win.

A good memory is fine - but the ability to forget is the true test of greatness.

Borrowing trouble from the future does not deplete the supply.

Strength is built when strength is tested. Don't lessen the lesson!

Confront improper conduct, not by retaliation, but by example.

It is easier to be critical than correct.

What you dislike in another, take care to correct in yourself.

Good manners are the small coin of virtue.

To belittle, is to be little.

True politeness is perfect ease and freedom; it simply consists in treating others just as you love to be treated yourself.

Practice an attitude of gratitude.

It is easy to tell a lie; but hard to tell just one lie.

No man has good enough memory to make a successful liar.

A problem honestly stated is half solved.

Honesty is always the best policy.

For students to experience growth, they must experience consequences. Teachers should establish a system of rules and consequences that will encourage thoughtful decision-making.

Laws too gentle are seldom obeyed; too severe, seldom executed.
    Benjamin Franklin

Every great mistake has a halfway moment; a split second, when it can be recalled and perhaps remedied.
    Pearl S. Buck

A man who refuses to admit his mistakes can never be successful.
    The Bible

The only thing necessary for the triumph of evil is for good men to do nothing.
    Edmund Burke

Every unpunished murder takes away something from the security of every man's life.
    Daniel Webster

When your neighbor's house is afire your own property is at stake.

Four things belong to a judge: to hear courteously, to answer wisely, to consider soberly, and to decide impartially.
    Socrates

Justice without force is powerless; force without justice is tyrannical.
    Blaise Pascal

Judge a tree from its fruit; not from the leaves.
    Euripides

Examine the contents, not the bottle.
    The Talmud

If you judge people, you have not time to love them.
    Mother Teresa

Worry is interest paid on trouble before it falls due.
    William Ralph Inge

People who fight fire with fire usually end up with ashes.
    Abigail Van Buren

Little strokes fell great oaks.

The experience of admitting wrongdoing clears the forest of deceit, paves the road of character, and opens up the wilderness to progress.

You observe a lot by watching.

Hear no evil, see no evil, speak no evil - and you'll never be invited to a party.

The best way to break a bad habit is to drop it.
    D. S. Yoder

He who conquers his anger conquers a strong enemy.

Whenever I've lost my temper, I've lost my reason too.

A hearty laugh gives one a dry cleaning, while a good cry is a wet wash.

The more things are forbidden, the more popular they become.

Forgiveness is not a feeling but a promise or commitment of three things:
1. I will not use it against them in the future.
2. I will not talk to others about them.
3. I will not dwell on it myself. Jay E. Adams

To speak ill of others is a dishonest way of praising ourselves.
    Ariel and Will Durant

The more reasonable we are in our expectations, the fewer disappointments we will have in life.
    A. Nielen

A good laugh and a long sleep are the best cures in the doctor's book.

I can live for two months on a good compliment.
    Mark Twain

It is easier to derail a runaway train than to stop it.

Changing one's attitude is always more successful than changing one's circumstances.

Control is to stress as water is to fire.

The fear of exposure often outweighs the necessity of correction.

Deflect anger and the aggressor will have spent his energy while you retain your balance. Attempt to stop the anger and a collision must result.

Truth may be stretched, but cannot be broken, and always gets above falsehood, as oil does above water.
    Miguel de Cervantes

As scarce as truth is, the supply has always been in excess of the demand.
    Josh Billings

Let a sleeping dog lie.

Making excuses doesn't change the truth.

Our minds possess by nature an insatiable desire to know the truth.
    Cicero

Wisdom knows no age and truth is truth no matter where you find it.
    H. Jackson Brown, Jr.

Truth cannot be killed with the sword nor abolished by law.

It is better to suffer for speaking the truth than that the truth should suffer for want of speaking it.

Truth is not only violated by falsehood; it may be equally outraged by silence.

Truth has to change hands only a few times to become fiction.

If you tell the truth, you don't have to remember anything.
    Mark Twain

Troubles like babies, grow larger by nursing them.
    Lady Holland

There's one thing to be said for inviting trouble; it generally accepts.
    May Maloo

One reason people get into trouble is that trouble usually starts out being fun.

There are people who are always anticipating trouble, and in this way they manage to enjoy many sorrows that never really happen to them.
    Josh Billings

If you would like to develop more patience, you should prepare for trouble.
    R. E. Phillips

One moment of patience may ward off great disaster; one moment of impatience may ruin a whole life.

Patience is something you admire in the driver behind you, but not in the one ahead.
    Bill McGlashen

When you come to the end of your rope, make a knot, and hang on.

Chapter 5

THE RUNGS OF THE LADDER OF SUCCESS
ARE NOT MEANT TO BE RESTED ON, BUT
TO SUPPORT US UNTIL WE ARE ABLE
TO CLIMB HIGHER.
ANONYMOUS

We live under the same sky, but we all have different horizons.

Great minds discuss ideas; Average minds discuss events; Small minds discuss people.

A contented person is one who enjoys the scenery along the detour.

Confidence is locking the door and then not trying the knob to be sure.

Perseverance is not a long race; it is many short races one after another.

If we appreciate what we have, it always becomes more. If we belittle what we have, it always becomes less.

Success is harnessing your heart to a task you love to do.

The most successful thing you can do in life is to figure out who you are and then be yourself.

Nothing we wear makes as much difference as the expression on our faces.

Obstacles are those things you see when you take your eyes off the goal.

Yesterday is a cancelled check; tomorrow is a promissory note; today is the only cash you have - so spend it wisely.
    Kay Lyons

You can't change the past but you can ruin the present by worrying over the future.

If you can find a path with no obstacles it probably doesn't lead anywhere.

Contentment consists not in great wealth but in few wants.

The rungs of the ladder of success are not meant to be rested on, but to support us until we are able to climb higher.

The door to the room of success swings on the hinges of determination.

If Columbus had turned back, no one would have blamed him. No one would remember him either.

When your dreams turn to dust, don't fret - vacuum.

Indecision is torture.

Some people treat obstacles as stumbling blocks; others treat them as stepping-stones.

Ambition is when your dreams put on work clothes.

Horizons mark the end of our sight and the beginning of our journeys.

The man who does nothing but wait for his ship to come in has already missed the boat.

Don't expect motivation to fall from the sky; it rises up from true grit.

I have unlimited potential and owe it to myself to live each day fully!
    C. L. Charles

Building self-esteem: There are extraordinary qualities in ordinary people.

A guide to building self-esteem:
Praise loudly; blame softly.

There is no easy road to success.

I am responsible for myself: I alone choose how I think, feel and act.
    C. L. Charles

Let me win. But if I cannot win, let me be brave in the attempt.

Use what talents you have. The woods would be very silent if no birds sang there except those that sang best.
    Henry Van Dyke

He who truly believes something is willing to act upon it.

It is never too late to be what you might have been.
    George Eliot

You see things; and you say, "Why?" But I dream things that never were; and I say, "Why not?"
    George Bernard Shaw

Our greatest glory consists not in never failing, but in rising every time we fall.
    Oliver Goldsmith

Don't be afraid of the space between your dreams and reality. If you can dream it, you can make it so.
    Belva Davis

People do not lack strength; they lack will.

I leave this rule for others, when I am dead. Be always sure you are right, then go ahead.
    Davy Crockett

Ah, but a man's reach should exceed his grasp, or what's a heaven for?
    Robert Browning

The poison of pessimism creates an atmosphere of wholesale negativism where nothing but the bad side of everything is emphasized.

Ambition and drive keep the successful person focused on what's ahead not on what has happened.

The quitter never wins. The winner never quits.

It is better to wear out than to rust out.

Never despair, but if you do, work on in despair.

The grass is greener on the other side, but it is just as hard to mow.

A smooth sea never makes a skillful mariner.

There are two ways of spreading light; to be the candle or the mirror that reflects it.
    Edith Wharton

Within your heart keep one still, secret spot where dreams may go.
    Louise Driscoll

Work is not the cause - Rest is not the cure.

The human race is divided into two classes - those who go ahead and do something and those who sit still and inquire why it wasn't done the other way.
    Oliver Wendell Holmes

In each man is a spark able to kindle new fires of human progress, new light for the human spirit.
    Charles A. Lindbergh

There's only one way to make dreams come true - Wake up and go to work.

Winning isn't everything . . . but wanting to win is.
    Vince Lombardi

Goals are like stars; they may not be reached, but they can always be a guide.

A goal is not a goal until it is written down.
    Matalie Goldberg

Youth must strive for goals afar, Which old men dare not try.

A sleeping fox catches no chickens.

What you do not start
You do not finish.

Greatness, after all, in spite of its name, appears to be not so much a certain size, as a certain quality in human lives.

Hitch your wagon to a star.
    Ralph Waldo Emerson

When you are through improving, you're through . . .

In every matter of right and wrong, we can't be neutral.
    Theodore Roosevelt

Whatever potential you have can be enhanced. Your accomplishments don't have to be earth shattering. Your own satisfaction is the most important thing.

Don't shirk
Your work
For the sake of a dream.
A fish
In the dish
Is worth two in the stream.

Perseverance is the one quality successful people share more than any other.

Great opportunities come to all, but many do not know they have met them.
    W. E. Dunning

Your attitude is vital to the outcome. Keep positive and be confident.
Choose to win and not to lose.

Life is a lot like tennis - the one who can serve best seldom loses.
    American Druggist

The problem is not the problem. The problem is my attitude about the problem.

Ability without ambition is like a car without a motor.

Imagination is the highest kite one can fly.
    Bacall

Never, never, never, never give up.
    Winston Churchill

A little dissatisfaction which every artist feels at the completion of a work forms the beginning of a new work.

I write when I'm inspired, and I see to it that I'm inspired at nine o'clock every morning.
    Peter de Vries

Challenges make you discover things about yourself that you never really knew. They're what make the instrument stretch - what make you go beyond the norm.
    Tyson

Don't judge those who try and fail. Judge only those who fail to try.

You can always tell luck from ability by its duration.

If A equals success, then the formula is A=X+Y+Z, with X being work, Y being play, and Z keeping your mouth shut.
    Albert Einstein

If you refuse to accept anything but the best, you very often get it.
    Somerset Maugham

There is no stigma attached to recognizing a bad decision in time to install a better one.
    Lawrence J. Peter

Good ideas need landing gear as well as wings.

The greater the obstacle the more glory in overcoming it.
    Moliere

Great hopes make great men.
    Thomas Fuller

The quality of a person's life is in direct proportion to his commitment to excellence, regardless of his chosen field of endeavor.
    Vince Lombardi

Excellence is never an accident.

Anything one man can imagine another can make real.
    Jules Verne

Reach high, for stars lie hidden in your soul. Dream deep, for every dream precedes the goal.
    Vaull Starr

To do for the world more than the world does for you - that is success.
    Henry Ford

The only true measure of success is the ratio between what we might have done on the one hand and the thing we have made of ourselves on the other.
    H. G. Wells

The talent of success is nothing more than doing what you can do well; and doing well whatever you do, without a thought of fame.
    Henry Wadsworth Longfellow

Success is never final, and failure never fatal.

Success is measured not so much by the position that one has reached in life, as by the obstacles which he has overcome while trying to succeed.
    Booker T. Washington

Behold the turtle: He makes progress only when he sticks his neck out.
    James Bryant Conant

The wise does at once what the fool does at last.
    Baltasar Gracian

A fella doesn't last long on what he has done; he has to keep delivering!

A rolling stone gathers no moss, but it obtains a certain polish.

The world stands aside to let anyone pass who knows where he is going.

The only thing you can give a man without hurting him is an opportunity.
    Henry Ford

A man in earnest finds means, or if he cannot find, creates them.
    W. E. Channing

I start where the last man left off.
    Thomas A. Edison

People are always blaming their circumstances for what they are. I don't believe in circumstances. The people who get on in this world are the people who get up and look for the circumstances they want, and if they can't find them, make them.
    George Bernard Shaw

A man's ambition should be high. Not scratched in dirt - carved in the sky.
    Thomas L. Forest

The poorest of all men is not the man without a cent; it is the man without a dream.

When you stop having dreams and ideals - well, you might as well stop altogether.

    Time is:
Too slow for those who wait, Too swift for those who fear, Too long for those who grieve, Too short for those who rejoice, But for those who love, time is not.
    Henry Van Dyke

The right way to kill time is to work it to death.
    R. G. LeTourneau

The proper function of a man is to live, not to exist. I shall not waste my days in trying to prolong them. I shall use my time.
    Jack London

Time - use it or lose it.

We always have time for the things we put first.

Most people get ahead during the time that others waste.

It takes as much time and energy to wish as it does to plan.

The greatest waste of energy is spent fleeing from the task.

The ache of unfulfilled dreams is the worst pain of all.

At some time in our life we feel a trembling, fearful longing to do some good thing. Life finds its noblest spring of excellence in this hidden impulse to do our best.
    Robert Collyer

The right angle to approach a difficult problem is the "try angle."

Kites rise highest against the wind - not with it.
    Winston Churchill

When you soar like an eagle, you attract hunters.
    Milton Gould

The slogan "Press on" has solved and always will solve the problems of the human race.
    Calvin Coolidge

When one door closes, another opens; but we often look so long and so regretfully upon the closed door that we do not see the one which has opened for us.
    Alexander Graham Bell

I always tried to turn every disaster into an opportunity.
    John D. Rockefeller

Positive anything is better than negative nothing.
    Elbert Hubbard

Consider the postage stamp, my son. It secures success through its ability to stick to one thing till it gets there.
    Josh Billings

Perseverance is a great element of success. If you only knock long enough and loud enough at the gate, you are sure to wake up somebody.
    Henry Wadsworth Longfellow

Do you see difficulties in every opportunity or opportunities in every difficulty?

Keep an open mind, but don't keep it too open or people will throw a lot of rubbish into it.

Our ship would come in much sooner if we'd swim out to meet it.

A good sleep and plenty of exercise changes many opinions.
    R. E. Phillips

Forget the past. No one becomes successful in the past.

The nearer any disease approaches to a crisis, the nearer it is to a cure. Danger and deliverance make their advances together; and it is only in the last push that one or the other takes the lead.
    Thomas Paine

There is no medicine like hope, no incentive so great, and no tonic so powerful as expectation of something better tomorrow.
    Orison Marden

The finest eloquence is that which gets things done.
    David Lloyd George

My interest is in the future because I will spend the rest of my life there.
    Charles F. Kettering

The world is blessed most by men who do things and not by those who merely talk about them.
    James Oliver

I never allow myself to become discouraged under any circumstances; The three great essentials to achieve anything worthwhile are, first, hard work; second, stick-to-itiveness; third, common sense.
    Thomas A. Edison

When life gives you lemons, make lemonade.

Do what is expected of you and you gain credibility. Don't do what is expected of you and you lose credibility.

If you've made up your mind that you can't do something - you're absolutely right!

Two men look out through the same bars;
One sees the mud, and one the stars.
    Frederick Langbridge

Why not go out on a limb? Isn't that where the fruit is?
    Frank Scully

If you are getting kicked from behind, it is because you are out in front.
    R. E. Phillips

Ability is of little account without opportunity.
    Napoleon Bonaparte

I came, I saw, I conquered.
    Julius Caesar

Humility is the greatest expression of confidence.

Sometimes it isn't safe to rock the boat, but if you want good things to happen, you've got to speak up.
    Donna K. Moffat

The higher you get the farther you see. Vision is most insightful when great obstacles have been conquered.

Possessing ambition leads to success. Being possessed by ambition leads to failure.

It is a great thing to do little things well.

People are in such a hurry to get to the "good life" that they often rush right past it.

Don't let what you cannot do interfere with what you can do.
    John Wooden

Nothing in the world can take the place of persistence . . . Persistence and determination alone are omnipotent.
    Calvin Coolidge

In the middle of difficulty lies opportunity.
    Albert Einstein

Life is like a scooter car; not much happens unless you do some peddling.

Every great achievement was once considered impossible.

I can change any time I choose to; I don't know what I can do until I try.
    C. L. Charles

Cheerfulness is the atmosphere in which all things thrive.
    Jean Paul Richter

Confidence or courage is conscious ability - the sense of power.
    William Hazlitt

Little minds are tamed and subdued by misfortune, but great minds rise above it.
    Washington Irving

Dare to be wise; He, who postpones the hour of living rightly is like the rustic who waits for the river to run out before he crosses.
    Horace

It is better to light one small candle than to curse the darkness.
    Confucius

It's not how far you fall, but how high you bounce.

If your live is free of failures, you're not taking enough risks.

I have lived eighty-six years. I have watched men climb to success, hundreds of them, and of all the elements that are important for success, the most important is faith. No great thing comes to any man unless he has courage.
    James Cardinal Gibbons

Nothing in the world can take the place of persistence. Talent will not; nothing is more common than unsuccessful men with talent. Genius will not; unrewarded genius is almost a proverb. Education will not; the world is full of educated failures. Persistence and determination alone are omnipotent.
    Calvin Coolidge

Two stonecutters were asked what they were doing. The first said, "I'm cutting this stone into blocks." The second replied, "I'm on a team that's building a cathedral."
    Old Story

When an archer misses the mark, he turns and looks for the fault within himself. Failure to hit the bulls-eye is never the fault of the target. To improve your aim - improve yourself.
    Gilbert Arland

Man's mind once stretched by a new idea, never regains its original dimension.
    Oliver Wendell Holmes

Imagination is more important than knowledge.
    Albert Einstein

Well done is better than well said.
    Benjamin Franklin

Never let a day go by without giving at least three people a compliment.

Chapter 6

**COMMITTING A GREAT TRUTH TO MEMORY IS ADMIRABLE;
COMMITTING IT TO LIFE IS WISDOM.
WILLIAM A. WARD**

The secret of patience is being able to do something else while waiting.

When no one listens, History repeats itself.

The only people who seem to have enough time are those who are serving it.

An assumption is the first ingredient for a disaster.

Waste of time is the most extravagant and costly of all expenses.

A stitch in time saves nine.

To travel, hopefully, is a better thing than to arrive.
    Stevenson

Live simple, love well and take time to smell the flowers along the way.

Never promise more than you can perform.

The art of being wise is the art of knowing what to overlook.
    William James

Character is like the foundation to a house - it is below the surface.

The straight and narrow path would not be so narrow if more people walked it.

People, who fly into a rage, always make a bad landing.

True wisdom lies in gathering precious moments out of each day.

Wisdom is knowing what to do next, skill is knowing how to do it, and virtue is doing it.
    David Starr Jordan

When a person is "a picture of health" one's very apt to find the setting for the picture is a happy frame of mind.

A joyous word may light the day; A timely word may lessen stress A loving word may heal and bless.

What we leave in our children is more important than what we leave to them.

Life is a coin. You can spend it any way you want to, but you can only spend it once.

Honesty is the first chapter of the book of wisdom.
    Thomas Jefferson

It is better to earn recognition without getting it, than to get recognition without earning it.

Do what is right (honest). It is the right thing to do. Do your very best at all things. Remember the Golden Rule; treat others as you'd like to be treated.
    Lou Holts

We are to invest, not waste the precious deposit into each day's account of 86,400 seconds, 1,440 minutes, 24 hours. We must spend them all the same day. We can not carry them over to the next.

A good laugh is sunshine in a house.
    William M. Thackeray

It is easy to dodge an elephant but not a fly.

For of all sad words of tongue or pen, The saddest are these; It might have been.
    John Greenleaf Whittier

Life is what happens while you are making other plans.
    John Lennon

Power corrupts, and absolute power corrupts absolutely.
    Lord John

The greatest wealth is good health.
    Emerson

If I am not satisfied with what I have, I will never be satisfied with what I want.

If you are too big to do little things, you are too little to do big things.

Men of ill judgment oft ignore the good that lies within their hands, till they have lost it.
    Sophocles

I define hate as "the means by which I punish and destroy myself for the actions of others."
    Dr. K. Olson

It is by those who have suffered that the world is most advanced.

They also serve, who only stand and wait.

I'm so accustomed to being tense that when I'm calm I get nervous.

If the world seems cold to you, kindle fires to warm it.
    Lucy Larcom

The man, who leaves home to set the world on fire, often comes back for more matches.

Think little of what others think of you.

He tried to be somebody by trying to be like everybody, which makes him a nobody.

The greatest pleasure I know is to do a kindness (good action) secretly, and have it found out accidentally.
    Charles Lamb

You cannot do a kindness too soon, because you never know how soon it will be too late.
    Old Proverb

Kindness is the sunshine in which virtue grows.
    Robert Ingersoll

Kindness and laughter translate into any language.

Talk to a man about himself, and he will listen for hours.

Think not of yourself more highly than you ought to think.
    The Bible

Pride makes us esteem ourselves; Vanity desires the esteem of others.

If it is doubtful, don't.

Everything has been thought of before, but the problem is to think of it again.
    Johann W. Von Goethe

Of all the things to wear, your expression is the most important.

A smile increases your face value.
Politeness is to do and say,
The kindest thing in the kindest way.

He, who buys what he does not want, will soon want what he cannot buy.

A dream and a star shine best from afar!
    Joan Walsh Anglund

We can easily forgive a child who is afraid of the dark; the real tragedy of life is when men are afraid of the light.
    Plato

How far the little candle throws his beams! So shines a good deed in a naughty world.
    William Shakespeare

It is not what you have that matters, It is what you do with what you have.

You give but little when you give of your possessions. It is when you give of yourself that you truly give.
    Kahil Gibran

I regret often that I have spoken; never that I have kept silent.
    Syrus

I expect to pass through this world but once. Any good therefore that I can do, or any kindness that I can show to any fellow creature let me do it now. Let me not defer or neglect it, for I shall not pass this way again.
    Stephen Grellet (Quaker)

Accept the situation or change it.

The web of our life is of a mingled yarn, good and ill together.
    William Shakespeare

Keep your face to the sunshine and you cannot see the shadow.
    Helen Keller

Who can separate his faith from his actions, or his belief from his occupations?
    Kahil Gibran

If a man measures life by what others do for him, he is going to be very disappointed; but if he measures life by what he does for others, there is no time for despair.

The opera's not over until the fat lady sings!

The law of nature says; You never get something without giving up something.

The future tense of "I give" is "I take."

If you want the rainbow, you must put up with the rain.
    Parton

The difference between a conviction and a prejudice is that you can explain a conviction without getting angry.

There is no right way to do a wrong thing.

Tact is the ability to close your mouth before someone else wants to.

The first step on the road to ruin is to forget God.

Even if you're on the right track, you'll get run over if you just sit there.
    Will Rogers

We can not lead someone else to the light while we are standing in the dark.

Common sense is not so common.

Oh, the difference between nearly right and exactly right.

Getting fired can be the best thing that can happen to you.

It is often the failure, who is the pioneer in new lands, new undertakings, and new forms of expression.
    Eric Hoffer

I have but one lamp by which my feet are guided and that is the lamp of experience. I know of no way of judging the future but by the past.
    Patrick Henry

Example is the best way of influencing others.

We make a living by what we get, but we make a life by what we give.
    Winston Churchill

There are no unimportant jobs, no unimportant people, and no unimportant acts of kindness.

Let the words I speak today be soft and tender, for tomorrow I may have to eat them!

Well done is better than well said.
    Benjamin Franklin

The point of having an open mind, like having an open mouth, is to close it on something solid.
    G. K. Chesterton

To God, thy country, and thy friend be true.
    Henry Vaughan

Eating words has never given me indigestion.
    Winston Churchill

Anytime you see a turtle up on top of a fence post, you know he had some help.
    Alex Haley

What we hope ever to do with ease, we must learn first to do with diligence.
    Samuel Johnson

The urge to quit is the signal that an opportunity to excel is at hand.

You shouldn't speak unless you can improve on the silence.

When you compete with yourself, you have a worthy adversary.

The denser the mass, the greater the force of gravity.

You're smart when you know the answer. You're wise when you know you do not.

Priorities are the traffic signals on the road of life.

Those who know the truth are not equal to those who love it.
    Confucius

Nothing is more beautiful than the loveliness of the woods before sunrise.
    George Washington Carver

We are living in a world of beauty but how few of us open our eyes to see it?
    Lorado Taft

Though we travel the world over to find the beautiful, we must carry it with us, or we find it not.
    Ralph Waldo Emerson

Dost thou love life? Then do not squander Time, for that's the stuff life is made of.
    Benjamin Franklin

Waste of wealth is sometimes retrieved; waste of health, seldom; but waste of time, never.
    Thomas Campion

Live every day of your life as though you expected to live forever.
    Douglas MacArthur

Truth is wherever you decide to face it.
    John Berry

No pleasure is comparable to standing upon the vantage-ground of truth.
    Francis Bacon

Some people pay a compliment as if they expected a receipt.
    Frank Hubbard

When I did well, I heard it never; When I did ill, I heard it ever.

The best throw of the dice is to throw them away.

I had no shoes and complained until I met a man who had no feet.

We find comfort among those who agree with us - growth among those who don't.
    Frank A. Clark

Character builds slowly, but it can be torn down with incredible swiftness.
    Faith Baldwin

The way to find out about one man, I have found, is to ask him about another.
    Gerard Fay

A celebrity is a person who works hard all his life to become well known, and then wears dark glasses to avoid being recognized.
    Fred Allen

The world hates change; yet it is the only thing that has brought progress.
    Charles Kettering

A bird in the hand is worth two in the bush.
    Cervantes

The most bored people in the world are not the underprivileged but the over- privileged.
    Fulton Sheen

To distrust is to be lonely.
    R. E. Phillips

Whenever a doctor cannot do good, he must be kept from doing harm.
    Hippocrates

If you don't scale the mountain, you can't see the view.

If you want to make enemies, try to change something.
    Woodrow Wilson

When I can't handle events, I let them handle themselves.
    Henry Ford

When good people in any country cease their vigilance and struggle, then evil men prevail.
    Pearl S. Buck

There is one thing stronger than all the armies in the world; and that is an idea whose time has come.
    Victor Hugo

The man with time to burn never gave the world any light.

Lost, yesterday, somewhere between sunrise and sunset, two golden hours, each set with sixty diamond minutes. No reward is offered for they are gone forever.
    Horace Mann

Repay evil with good and you deprive the evildoer of all the pleasure of his wickedness.
    Leo Tolstoy

The first great gift we can bestow on others is a good example.
    Thomas Morell

Example is not the main thing in influencing others. It is the only thing.
    Albert Schweitzer

Wisdom outweighs any wealth.
    St. Clement of Rome

If your outgo exceeds your income, your upkeep will be your downfall.
    John Poure

I've a grand memory for forgetting.
    Robert Louis Stevenson

Personal liberty is the paramount essential to human dignity and human happiness.
    Bulwer Lytton

You only keep what you give away.
    R. E. Phillips

If you have much, give of your wealth; If you have little, give of your heart.

The poorest man would not part with health for money, but the richest would gladly part with all his money for health.
    C. C. Colton

Laughter is the shortest distance between two people.
    Victor Borge

He who laughs . . . lasts.
    Mary P. Poole

It doesn't matter what you do as long as you're the boss.

Great minds have purposes, others have wishes.
    Washington Irving

The hero is no braver than an ordinary man, but he is brave five minutes longer.
    Ralph Waldo Emerson

The doors of wisdom are never shut.
    Benjamin Franklin

A grain of gold will gild a great surface, but not so much as a grain of wisdom.
    Henry David Thoreau

Wisdom is the highest virtue, and it has in it four other virtues; of which one is prudence, another temperance, the third fortitude, the fourth justice.
    Boethius

The invariable mark of wisdom is to see the miraculous in the common.
    Ralph Waldo Emerson

I begin to suspect that a man's bewilderment is the measure of his wisdom.
    Nathaniel Hawthorne

Wisdom is that olive that springeth from the heart, bloometh on the tongue, and beareth fruit in the actions.
    Elizabeth Grymeston

There is four hundred times as much learning in the world as there is wisdom.
    Josh Billings

The wisest mind hath something yet to learn.
    George Santayana

The farther backward you can look, the farther forward you are likely to see.
    Winston Churchill

The greatest good is wisdom.
    St. Augustine

Of all human pursuits the pursuit of wisdom is the most perfect, the most sublime, the most profitable, the most delightful.
    St. Thomas Aquinas

Lost time is never found again.

Wisdom is of the soul, is not susceptible of proof, is its own proof.
    Walt Whitman

I never think of the future. It comes soon enough.
    Albert Einstein

Humanity is just a work in progress.
    Tennessee Williams

The only medicine for suffering, crime, and all the other woes of mankind, is wisdom.
    Thomas H. Huxley

A wise man who stands firm is a statesman, a foolish man who stands firm is a catastrophe.
    Adlai Stevenson

Anytime a man takes a stand, there'll come a time when he'll be tested to see how firm his feet are planted.

To flee vice is the beginning of virtue, and to have got rid of folly is the beginning of wisdom.
    Horace

All men desire peace; however, few desire the things which make for peace.

The grinding that would wear away to nothing a lesser stone, merely serves to give luster to a diamond.

The worst of men often give the best advice.

Virtue lies in the struggle, not in the prize.

Sincerity is all we need to help us do a friendly deed.

Kindness is indeed sublime and worth the trouble anytime.

He conquers who endures.

No service is too small and none too great, from the giving of a cup of cold water to the laying down of one's life.

The best way to succeed in life is to act on the advice you give to others.

We are each burdened with prejudice; against the poor or the rich, the smart or the slow, the gaunt or the obese. It is natural to develop prejudices. It is noble to rise above them.

You can't do anything about the length of your life; But you can to something about its width and depth.

When you are healthy all other problems of life appear insignificant.
    Louise Lague

While in the race to save our face, why not conquer the inner space?

He that falls in love with himself will have no rival.
    Benjamin Franklin

Hit the ball over the fence and you can take your time going around the bases.
    John W. Raper

It is not the going out of port, but the coming in, that determines the success of a voyage.
Henry Ward Beecher

Try not to become a man of success but rather try to become a man of value.
    Albert Einstein

We have fifty million reasons for failure, but not a single excuse.
    Rudyard Kipling

There was never a person who did anything worth doing that did not receive more than he gave.
    Henry Ward Beecher

The greatest undeveloped territory in the world lies under your hat.

A man's virtues should not be measured by his occasional exertions but by his ordinary days.
    Will Rogers

We aspire by setting up ideals and striving after them.
    Harry Emerson Fosdick

He, who wants to get to the top, must first get off his bottom.

No matter what your lot in life, build something on it.

Anybody who thinks talk is cheap should get some legal advice.
    Franklin P. Jones

With the fearful strain that is on me night and day, if I did not laugh I should die.
    Abraham Lincoln

The penalty of leadership is loneliness.
    H. Wheeler Robinson

You never realize what a good memory you have until you try to forget something.

Necessity is the mother of invention.

It is better to be faithful than to be famous.
    Theodore Roosevelt

He that lacks time to mourn, lacks time to mend.
    Sir Henry Taylor

Sometimes one pays most for the things one gets for nothing.
    Albert Einstein

Wishes never filled the bag. With wishing comes grieving.

Committing a great truth to memory is admirable; committing it to life is wisdom.
    William A. Ward

Wise men are not always silent, but know when to be.

Where there is a will, there's a way.

Pain makes man think. Thought makes man wise. Wisdom makes life endurable.
    John Patrick

All you have to do to lose weight is mix plenty of self-control with everything you eat!

Choose a wife rather by your ear than your eye.

Brevity is the soul of wit.
    William Shakespeare

Justice is truth in action.
    Joubert

A jury consists of twelve persons chosen to decide who has the better lawyer.
    Robert Frost

Good judgment comes from experience; and experience, well that comes from bad judgment.

Junk is something you keep for years and then throw out two weeks before you need it.

Imitation is the sincerest form of flattery.

A diamond is a chunk of coal that made good under pressure.

You can fool too many of the people too much of the time.
    James Thurber

Poverty may teach us to sink or swim.

He who gets someone else to blow his horn will find that the sound travels twice as far.

The measure of a man is what he does with power.
    Pittacus

Patience and gentleness is power.
    Leigh Hunt

Character is power.
    Booker T. Washington

No man ever injured his eyesight by looking on the bright side of things.

Heroism consists in hanging on one minute longer.

The past always looks better than it was.
    Finley P. Dunne

All the king's horses and all the king's men can't put the past together again.
    Dale Carnegie

The world is round and the place, which may seem like the end may also be the beginning.
    Ivy Baker Priest

Not everyone repeats gossip. Some improve it.
    Franklin P. Jones

Those who had free seats at a play hiss first.

The secret of contentment is knowing how to enjoy what you have, and to be able to lose all desire for things beyond your reach.
    Lin Yutang

I would rather appreciate the things I do not have than to have things I do not appreciate.

When a thing ceases to be a subject of controversy, it ceases to be a subject of interest.
    William Hazlitt

You can't appreciate home until you've left it, money till it's spent, your wife till she joined a woman's club, and Old Glory till you see it hanging on a broomstick of a counsul in a foreign town.
    O Henry

The search for happiness is one of the chief sources of unhappiness.
    Eric Hoffer

Appearances deceive; men are not always what they seem to be.

A good horse never lacks a saddle.

There's nothing so annoying as arguing with a person who knows what he is talking about.

Arguing is a game that two can play at. But it is a strange game in that neither opponent ever wins.
    Benjamin Franklin

To look up and not down,
To look forward and not back, To look out and not in, and To lend a hand.
    Edward Everett Hale

A defeat may be a victory in disguise.

What men value in the world is not rights, but privileges.
    H. L. Mencken

A man never knows what a fool he is until he hears himself imitated by one.
    Herbert Tree

April 1st is the day upon which we are reminded of what we are on the other 364.
    Mark Twain

No person was ever honored for what he received. Honor has been the reward for what he gave.
    Calvin Coolidge

It is one of the most beautiful compensations of this life that no man can sincerely try to help another without helping himself.
    Emerson

The biggest liar in the world is -"They Say."
    Douglas Malloch

The liar's punishment is not in the least that he is not believed but that he cannot believe anyone else.
    George Bernard Shaw

This is the punishment of a liar; they are not believed, even when they are telling the truth.
    The Talmud

If you tell the truth, you don't have to remember anything.
    Mark Twain

No legacy is so rich as honesty.
    William Shakespeare

When the truth is in your way, you are on the wrong road.
    Josh Billings

No one can disgrace us but ourselves.
    J. G. Holland

The reputation of a thousand years may be determined by the conduct of one hour.
    Japanese Proverb

Nothing astonishes men so much as common sense and plain dealing.
    Ralph Waldo Emerson

The real problem with your leisure is how to keep other people from using it.

To do nothing is in every man's power.
    Samuel Johnson

Nothing is said which has not been said before.

It takes a great man to make a good listener.
    Sir Arthur Helps

No man would listen to you talk if he didn't know it was his turn next.
    Edgar Watson Howe

Keep your fears to yourself, but share your courage with others.
    Robert Louis Stevenson

Fatigue is the best pillow.
    Benjamin Franklin

Fame is proof that the people are gullible.
    Emerson

Fame is a fickle food upon a shifting plate.
    Emily Dickinson

Familiarity breeds contempt.
    Publilius Syrus

Though familiarity may not breed contempt, it takes off the edge of admiration.
    William Hazlitt

He who gambles picks his own pockets.

The person who does not find time for exercise may have to find time for illness.

A person who represents himself has a fool for a client.

When a thing has been said and said well, have no scruple; Take it and copy it.
    Anatole France

You'll never find in a park or a city, a monument to a committee.
    Victoria Pasternak

Committee - a group of people who keep minutes and waste hours.
    Milton Berle

I hate being placed on committees. They are always having meetings, at which half are absent and the rest late.
    Oliver Wendel I. Holmes, Jr.

Commitment: The ability to bind oneself emotionally and intellectually to an idea or task that needs to be completed.

Taking something from one man and making it worse is plagiarism.
    George Moore

Endure and persist; this pain will turn to your good.
    Ovid

It is later than you think.

Time flies. It's up to you to be the navigator.
    Robert Orben

A stitch in time saves nine.

Without time, everything good and bad would happen at once. Trouble would worsen and joy would blur.
    R. E. Phillips Haste makes waste.

Dost thou love life? Then do not squander time, for that is the stuff life is made of.
    Benjamin Franklin

Our greatest danger in life is in permitting the urgent things to crowd out the important.
    Charles E. Humel

If everybody thought before they spoke, the silence would be deafening.
    Gerald Barzan

In times like these, it helps to recall that there have always been times like these.
    Paul Harvey

We live in the midst of alarms; anxiety beclouds the future; we expect some new disaster with each newspaper we read.
    Abraham Lincoln

In my belief, you cannot deal with the most serious things in the world unless you also understand the most amusing.
    Winston Churchill

The strongest principle of growth lies in human choice.
    George Eliot

Take time to smell the roses.

It always looks the darkest just before it gets totally black.
    Charlie Brown

As long as you laugh at your troubles, you may be sure that you will never run out of something to laugh at.

No one is more exasperating than the guy who can always see the bright side of our misfortunes.

Everything comes to him who hustles while he waits.
    Thomas A. Edison

The misfortunate thing about this world is that good habits are so much easier to give up than bad ones.
    Somerset Maugham

There are a lot of people in this world who spend so much time watching their health that they haven't the time to enjoy it.
    Josh Billings

The most pathetic person in the world is someone who has sight, but has no vision.
    Helen Keller

Truth is generally the best vindication against slander.
    Abraham Lincoln

Truth often suffers more by the heat of its defenders, than from the arguments of its opposers.
    William Penn

Men occasionally stumble over the truth, but most of them pick themselves up and hurry off as if nothing had happened.
    Winston Churchill

Chapter 7

**MOST PEOPLE GET AHEAD DURING
THE TIME THAT OTHERS WASTE.
ANONYMOUS**

Take yourself lightly and your job in life seriously.

The secret of happy living is not to do what you like but like what you do.

Find out what you like doing best - and get someone to pay you for doing it.
    Katherine Whitehorn

There is a time when you have to separate yourself from what other people expect of you, and do what you love. Because if you find yourself fifty years old and you aren't doing what you love - then, what's the point?
    Jim Carrey

April 15th:
Three hundred sixty-five days in the year you work like the dickens to make it and just when you're ready to start eating steady the government's ready to take it.

It's not the number of hours you put in, but what you put in the hours that count.

Just about the time you think you can make both ends meet, somebody moves the ends.

The surest way to go broke is to sit around waiting for a break.

Those who won't mind their own business, soon have no business to mind.

The secret of business is to know something that nobody else knows.
    Aristotle Onassis

Some live without working and others work without living.

Work is the greatest thing in the world, so we should save some of it for tomorrow.

Leisure is fun only when you can relax without feeling guilty knowing that you've earned a good rest.

A good vacation is over when you begin to yearn for work.

We often seem more anxious to defend our performance than to improve it.
    Cullen Hightower

It's not work that makes you tired, It's frustration that comes from lack of accomplishment.

The right attitude toward work multiplies achievement.

We must have a balanced life; Physical balance, Work balance, and Spiritual balance. Make time for friendships and family. Focus on relationships not on things.

To work and do your best will develop in you a hundred virtues which the idle never know.

No man needs sympathy because he has to work . . . Far and away the best prize that life has to offer is the chance to work hard at work worth doing.
    Theodore Roosevelt

To love life through labor is to be intimate with life's inmost secret.
    Kahlil Gibran

There is no substitute for hard work as a cure for worrying; work is better than whiskey.
    Thomas Edison

Everything comes to him who waits, if he works while he waits.

Every job is a self-portrait of the person who did it.

Work well done is art.

There are no unimportant jobs, no unimportant people, no unimportant acts of kindness.

No one can arrive from being talented alone. God gives talent; work transforms talent into genius.
    Pavlova

The biggest mistake you can make is to believe that you work for someone else.

I have discovered the secret of happiness - it is work, either with the hands or the head - something to do. It is the only safe and sure ground of happiness.
    John Burroughs

Nothing is more fun than a job you enjoy.

It's best not to quit at quitting time.

I don't pity any man who does hard work worth doing. I admire him. I pity the creature who doesn't work, at whichever end of the social scale he may regard himself as being.
    Theodore Roosevelt

I never did anything worth doing by accident, nor did any of my inventions come by accident; they came by hard work.
    Thomas Edison

Work is the ethic of equality.

Management is the secret of productivity.

No good ever comes of leisure idly spent; And heaven never helps the man who will not work.
    Sophocles

The highest reward for man's toil is not what he gets for it but what he becomes by it.
    John Ruskin

Patience is a most necessary qualification for business; many a man would rather you heard his story than granted his request.
    Lord Chesterfield

Sometimes the best deals are the ones you don't make.

If you hire mediocre people, they will hire mediocre people.

Whoever loves money never has money enough, whoever loves wealth is never satisfied with his income.
    The Bible

The wonderful thing about money is that it goes with any outfit you wear.

The most popular labor-saving device today is still a husband with money.
    July Adams

Win by persuasion, not by force.

If women didn't exist, all the money in the world would have no meaning.
    Aristotle Onassis

The secret of success is hard work.

The early bird gets the worm. The early bird gets the firm.

Small opportunities are often the beginning of great enterprises.
    Demosthenes

In the middle of difficulty lies opportunity.
    Albert Einstein

If you are looking for a big opportunity, seek out a big problem.

A wise man will make more opportunities than he finds.
    Francis Bacon

Don't wait for your ship to come in. Row out to meet it.

The beauty of work depends upon the way we meet it, whether we arm ourselves each morning to attack it as an enemy that must be vanquished before night comes - or whether we open our eyes with the sunrise to welcome it as an approaching friend who will keep us delightful company and who will make us feel at evening that the day was well worth its fatigue.
    Lucy Larcom

He has half the deed done, who has made a beginning.
    Horace

JOB = Just over broke.
    Bud Leftbridge

So much of what we call management consists in making it difficult for people to work.
    Peter Drucker

If you aren't fired with enthusiasm, you will be fired with enthusiasm.
    Vince Lombardi

Regardless of what company you work for, never forget the most important product you're selling is yourself.

When you dance with your customer, let him lead.

If once you forfeit the confidence of your fellow citizens, you can never regain their respect and esteem.
    Abraham Lincoln

I am only one; but still I am one. I cannot do everything, but still I can do something; I will not refuse to do the something I can do.
    Helen Keller

Societies can be no more stable than the social foundation on which they sit.
    Dr. James Dobson

Send these, the homeless, tempest- tossed to me. I lift my lamp beside the golden door!
    Emma Lazarus - Statue of Liberty

A system of justice can be no better than the value system it represents.

Can you show me where any society in human history has taxed itself into prosperity?
    Rush Limbaugh

Challenges can be stepping stones or stumbling blocks. It's just a matter of how you view them.

The closest we ever come to perfection is when we write our resumes.

Choose a job you love, and you will never have to work a day in your life.
    Confucius

You never get a second chance to make a good first impression.

Wealthy people miss one of life's great thrills - making the last car payment.

The one predominant duty is to find one's work and do it.
    Charlotte P. Gilman

No one ever went broke saving money.

Waste of time is the most extravagant and costly of all expenses.

Counting time is not so important as making time count.
    James J. Walker

The only people who seem to have enough time are those who are serving it.

There is more to life than increasing its speed.
    Mahatma Gandi

Time is life. To waste your time is to waste your life. To master time is to master your life.

We make a living by what we get, but we make a life by what we give.
    Winston Churchill

To understand the value of a month, ask the mother of a premature baby.

How well do you manage your time?

A creative organizer creates an organization that can function well without him.

The time to relax is when you don't have time for it.
    Sydney J. Harris

Time is a dressmaker specializing in alterations.
    Faith Baldwin

For most people the past pushes and the future pulls but nowhere is there a present to feel at ease in.
    Dick Seeger

Nothing gives a man more leisure time than being punctual.

If you use your time to improve yourself, you will not have the time to criticize others.

The person, who is always finding fault, seldom finds anything else.

Freedom means choosing your burden.

Make the mistakes of yesterday your lessons for today.

Unless we stand for something, we will fall for anything.

Compromise makes a good umbrella, but a poor roof.

Learn to break the tensions of daily living or the tensions will break you.

Failure is success if we learn from it.
    Malcomb S. Forbes

Success is not arriving at the summit of a mountain as a final destination. It is a continuing upward spiral of progress.

Success is harnessing your heart to a task you love to do.

Success is a ladder that cannot be climbed with your hands in your pockets.

Success is having the courage to meet failure without being defeated. It is refusing to let present loss interfere with your long-range goal.

Success is best measured by how far you've come with the talents you've been given.

Behind every successful man stands a proud wife and a surprised mother-in-law.
    Brooks Hays

He has achieved success who has lived well, laughed often, and loved much.
    Bessie Anderson Stanley

The true measure of success is not what you have, but what you can do without.

Success is getting what you want. Happiness is liking what you get.

When ask what makes a person successful? Eighty percent listed enthusiasm as the most important quality.

Excellence is never an accident.

Oh, the difference between nearly right and exactly right.

Praise in public. Criticize in private.

Don't let what you cannot do interfere with what you can do.
    John Wooden

The harder you work, the luckier you get.
    Gary Player

Winning is not a sometime thing; it's an all-time thing. You don't win once in a while, you don't do things right once in a while, you do them right all the time.
Winning is a habit. Unfortunately, so is losing.
    Vince Lombardi

Pride makes us do things well. But it is love that makes us do them to perfection.

Trust men and they will be true to you; treat them greatly and they will show themselves great.
    Ralph Waldo Emerson

When the One Great Scorer comes to write against your name, He marks, not that you won or lost, but how you played the game.
    Grantland Rice

What Went Wrong?
This is the story of four people: Everybody, Somebody, Anybody, and Nobody. There was an important job to be done and Everybody was sure that Somebody would do it. Anybody could have done it but Nobody did it.
Somebody got angry because it was Everybody's job. Everybody thought that Somebody would do it. But Nobody asked Anybody. It ended up that the job wasn't done and Everybody blamed Everybody, when actually Nobody asked Anybody.

PART TWO

THE MAKING OF A GREAT NATION

POSTERITY - YOU WILL NEVER KNOW HOW
MUCH IT HAS COST MY GENERATION TO
PRESERVE YOUR FREEDOM. I HOPE YOU
WILL MAKE GOOD USE OF IT.
JOHN QUINCY ADAMS

Chapter 1

**AMERICA! AMERICA! GOD SHED HIS GRACE
ON THEE AND CROWN THY GOOD WITH
BROTHERHOOD FROM SEA TO SHINING SEA!
KATHERINE LEE BATES**

The things that will destroy America are prosperity-at-any-price, safety-first instead of duty-first, the love of soft living, and the get-rich-quick theory of life.
    Theodore Roosevelt

There is nothing wrong with America that the love of freedom, intelligence, faith and energy of her citizens can not cure.
    Dwight D. Eisenhower

There is nothing wrong with America that together we can't fix.
    Ronald Reagan

O beautiful for spacious skies, For amber waves of grain,
For purple mountain majesties Above the fruited plain . . .
    Katherine Lee Bates

America! America!
  God shed his grace on thee
And crown thy good with brotherhood
  From sea to shining sea!
    Katherine Lee Bates

I am certain that, however great the hardships and the trials which loom ahead, our America will endure and the cause of human freedom will triumph.
    Cordell Hull

I would not hesitate to say that the United States is the finest society on a grand scale that the world has thus far produced.
    Alfred North Whitehead

Our country, right or wrong; When right, to be kept right; when wrong, to be put right.
    Carl Schurz

America is too great for small dreams.
    Ronald Reagan

America calls for government with a soul.
    Franklin D. Roosevelt

An American is one who will sacrifice property, ease and security in order that he and his children may retain the rights of free men.
    Harold L. Ickes

It is to the United States that all free men must look for the light and the hope of the world. Unless we dedicate ourselves completely to this struggle, unless we combat hunger with food, fear with trust, suspicion with faith, fraud with justice - and threats with power - nations will surrender to the futility, the panic, on which wars are fed.
    General Omar Bradley

Americanism is a question of principle, of purpose, of idealism, of character; it is not a matter of birthplace or creed, or line of descent.

Just what is it that America stands for? If she stands for one thing more than another it is for the sovereignty of self- governing people.
    Woodrow Wilson

America is not a mere body of traders; it is a body of free men. Our greatness is built upon our freedom - is moral, not material. We have a great ardor for gain; but we have a deep passion for the rights of man.
    Woodrow Wilson

An American is one who will fight for his freedom and that of his neighbor.
    Harold L. Ickes

To be an American is of itself almost a moral condition, an education, and a career.
    George Santayana

So it's home again, and home again,
America for me,
My heart is turning home again, and there I long to be.
    Henry Van Dyke

What are the American ideals? They are the development of the individual through liberty and the attainment of the common good through democracy and social justice.
    Louis D. Brandeis

When an American says he loves his country, he means not only that he loves the New England hills, the prairies glistening in the sun, the wide and rising plains, the great mountains, and the sea. He means that he loves the inner air, an inner light in which freedom lives and in which a man can draw a breath of self-respect.
    Adlai Stevenson

America lives in the heart of every man everywhere who wishes to find a region where he will be free to work out his destiny as he chooses.
    Woodrow Wilson

So, then, to every man his chance - to every man, regardless of his birth, his shining, golden opportunity - to every man the right to live, to work, to be himself, and to become whatever thing his manhood and his vision can combine to make him - this, seeker, is the promise of America.
    Thomas Wolfe

Go West, young man, and grow up with the country.
    Horace Greeley 1850

This is America . . . a brilliant diversity spread like stars, like a thousand points of light in a broad and peaceful sky.
    George Bush

When people start standing in line to get out of this country instead of standing in line to get in, then we can start worrying about our system.
    Bernard Baruch

I hope future ages will quote our proceedings with applause. It is one of the great duties of the democratical part of the constitution to keep itself pure. It is known in my Province that some other Colonies are not so numerous or rich as they are. I am for giving all the satisfaction in my power. The distinctions between Virginians, Pennsylvanians, New Yorkers, and New Englanders, are no more. I am not a Virginian, but an American.
    Patrick Henry 1774

The only foes that threaten America are the enemies at home, and these are ignorance, superstition, and incompetence.
    Elbert Hubbard

If America ever passes out as a great nation, we ought to put on our tombstone: America died from a delusion she had moral leadership.
    Will Rogers

There can be no fifty-fifty Americanism in this country. There is room here for only hundred-percent Americanism.
    Theodore Roosevelt

America is still the land of opportunity. Where else could you earn enough to owe so much?

I don't think it does any harm just once in a while to acknowledge that the whole country isn't in flames, that there are people in the country besides politicians, entertainers, and criminals.
    Charles Kuralt

Chapter 2

OUR GOVERNMENT IS THE POTENT,
THE OMNIPRESENT TEACHER. FOR GOOD OR ILL,
IT TEACHES THE WHOLE PEOPLE BY ITS EXAMPLE.
MCVEIGH

The Constitution only guarantees the American people the right to pursue happiness. You have to catch it yourself.
    Benjamin Franklin

Government is a trust, and the officers of the government are trustees; and both the trust and the trustees are created for the benefit of the people.
    Henry Clay

My experience in government is that when things are non-controversial, beautifully coordinated, and all the rest, it must be that there is not much going on.
    John F. Kennedy

Why has government been instituted at all? Because the passions of men will not conform to the dictates of reason and justice, without constraint.
    Alexander Hamilton

Govern yourself and you can govern the world.

The impersonal hand of government can never replace the helping hand of a neighbor.
    Hubert Humphrey

The whole government consists in the art of being honest.
    Thomas Jefferson

It's a good thing we don't get all the government we pay for.

There's no trick to being a humorist when you have the whole government working for you.
    Will Rogers

No nation was ever ruined by trade.
    Benjamin Franklin

When a man assumes a public trust, he should consider himself as public property.
    Thomas Jefferson

If the Government is big enough to give you everything you want, it is big enough to take away everything you have.
    Gerald Ford 1960

My reading of history convinces me that most bad government has grown out of too much government.
    John Sharp Williams

Everyone wants to live at the expense of the state. They forget that the state lives at the expense of everyone.
    Frederic Bastiat

Too bad that all the people who know how to run the country are busy driving taxicabs and cutting hair.
    George Burns

The ten most terrifying words in the English language are "I'm from the government and I'm here to help you."

The best minds are not in government. If any were, business would hire them away.
    Ronald Reagan

The single most exciting thing you encounter in government is competence, because it is so rare.
    Daniel Patrick Moynihan

Trying to make things work in government is sometimes like trying to sew a button on a custard pie.
    Admiral Hyman G. Rickover

The more corrupt the state, the more numerous the laws.

One of the greatest delusions in the world is the hope that the evils in this world are to be cured by legislation.
    Thomas B. Reed

A wise and frugal government, which shall restrain men from injuring one another, which shall leave them other- wise free to regulate their own pursuits of industry and improvement, and shall not take from the mouth of labor the bread it has earned, This is the sum of good government.
    Thomas Jefferson 1801

Any time we deny any citizen the full exercise of his Constitutional rights, we are weakening our own claim to them.
    Dwight D. Eisenhower

In politics, the middle way is none at all.
    John Adams 1776

The buck stops here.
    Harry S. Truman

Nothing is easier than the expenditure of public money. It doesn't appear to belong to anyone. The temptation is overwhelming to bestow it on somebody.
    Calvin Coolidge

I pledge you, I pledge myself, to a new deal for the American people.
    Franklin Roosevelt 1932

When you think of the government debt the next generation must pay off, it's no wonder the baby yells when it's born.

Power is a great aphrodisiac.
    Henry Kissinger 1971

Speak softly and carry a big stick; you will go far.
    Theodore Roosevelt 1903

The government is my shepherd I need not work. It alloweth me to lie down on a good job, it leadeth me beside still factories; it destroyeth my initiative. It leadeth me in the path of a parasite for politics' sake. Yea, though I walk through the valley of laziness and deficit spending, I will fear no evil, for the government is with me. It prepareth an economic Utopia for me by appropriating the earnings of my grandchildren. It filleth my head with false security. Surely the government should care for me all the days of my life and I shall dwell in a fool's paradise forever.

The history of Liberty is a history of limitations of governmental power, not the increase of it. When we resist, therefore, the concentration of power, we are resisting the powers of death, because concentration of power is what always precedes the destruction of human liberties.
    Woodrow Wilson

In this world nothing can be said to be certain, except death and taxes.
    Benjamin Franklin

I am tired of hearing that democracy doesn't work - it isn't supposed to work. We are supposed to work it.
    Alexander Woolcott

Democracy is based upon the conviction that there are extraordinary possibilities in ordinary people.
    Harry Emerson Fosdick

Democracy does not guarantee equality, only equality of opportunity.
    Irvin Kristol

The greatest blessing of our democracy is freedom. But in the last analysis, our only freedom is the freedom to discipline ourselves.
    Bernard Baruch

The great thing about living in a democracy is that you can say what you think without thinking.
    Dwight D. Eisenhower

Man's capacity for justice makes democracy possible, but man's inclination to injustice makes democracy necessary.

Democracy is not a fragile flower: still it needs cultivating.
    Ronald Reagan

Two cheers for democracy: one because it admits variety and two because it permits criticism.
    E. M. Forster

One of the most difficult decisions the individual in a democracy faces is whether or not he should forgo an immediate personal gain or advantage for the good of his country.
    Dwight D. Eisenhower

Bureaucracy defends the status quo long past time when the quo has lost its status.
    Lawrence J. Peter

The capitalist system does not guarantee that everybody will become rich, but it guarantees that anybody can become rich.
    Raul R. de Sales

Capitalism is the best means ever found to motivate men.

The inherent vice of capitalism is the unequal sharing of blessings; the inherent vice of socialism is the equal sharing of miseries.
    Winston Churchill

When I was a boy I was told that anyone could be president. I'm beginning to believe it.
    Clarence Darrow

My movements to the chair of government will be accompanied by feelings not unlike those of a culprit who is going to the place of his execution.
    George Washington

No man will ever bring out of the presidency the reputation, which carries him into it.
    Thomas Jefferson

Seriously, I do not think I am fit for the presidency.
    Abraham Lincoln

The four most miserable years of my life . . .
    John Adams

Within the first few months I discovered that being a president is like riding a tiger. A man has to keep riding or be swallowed.
    Harry S. Truman

I brought myself down, I gave them a sword and they stuck it in.
    Richard Nixon

From forty to sixty percent of the presidential office is not in administration but in morals, politics, and spiritual leadership. . .
As President of the United States and servant of God, he has much more to do than to run a desk at the head of the greatest corporation in the world. He has to guide a people in the greatest adventure ever undertaken on the planet.
    William Allen White

A politician is a man who shakes your hand before election and your confidence afterward.

In crime, they say take the money and run. In politics, they say run, then take the money.

I wouldn't call him a cheap politician. He's costing the country a fortune!

Too often foreign aid is when the poor people of a rich nation send their money to the rich people of a poor nation.

We can see these symptoms of materialism throughout our society, but the most visible one is loss of courage. People stand by and watch a fellow citizen being beaten or stabbed and they do not interfere, they are afraid. Our political leaders watch communism gobble up other nations and they do nothing. They are afraid. People complain in private about the state of affairs but will not speak out in public. They are afraid . . .
    General Lewis W. Walt

History is the discovering of the constant and universal principles of human nature.
    David Hume

It is not the neutrals or the lukewarms who make history.
    Adolf Hitler

History teaches us that man never learns from history.

Any event, once it has occurred, can be made to appear inevitable by some competent historian.
    Lee Simonson

Laws are like cobwebs, which may catch small flies, but let wasps and hornets break through.
    Jonathan Swift

The broad mass of a nation . . . will more easily fall victim to a big lie than a small one.
    Adolf Hitler

To educate a person in mind and not in morals is to educate a menace to society.

Our government is the potent, the omnipresent teacher. For good or ill, it teaches the whole people by its example.
    McVeigh

Chapter 3

**FREEDOM IS LIKE A COIN. IT HAS THE WORD PRIVILEGE
ON ONE SIDE AND RESPONSIBILITY ON THE OTHER.
JOSEPH SIZOO**

God grants liberty only to those who love it, and are always ready to guard and defend it.
    Daniel Webster

The condition upon which God has given liberty to man is eternal vigilance.
    John Philpot Curran

Proclaim liberty throughout all the land unto all the inhabitants thereof.
    Taken from Leviticus 25:10
    Liberty Bell Inscription

The God, who gave us life, gave us liberty at the same time. Can a nation be secure when we have removed a conviction that these liberties are the gift of God?
    Thomas Jefferson

Is life so dear, or peace so sweet, as to be purchased at the price of chains and slavery? Forbid it, Almighty God! I know not what course others may take; but as for me, give me liberty, or give me death!
    Patrick Henry (Virginian Patriot)

Together, we can keep America the shining light of liberty God intended it to be.
    Ronald Reagan 1984

The people have a right to the truth as they have a right to life, liberty and the pursuit of happiness.
    Frank Norris

Liberty is the only thing you cannot have unless you are willing to give it to others.
    William Allen White

The ground of liberty must be gained by inches.
    Thomas Jefferson

Liberty, when it begins to take root, is a plant of rapid growth.
    George Washington

Liberty means responsibility. That is why most men dread it.
    George Bernard Shaw

Eternal vigilance is the price of liberty.
    W. Phillips

When liberty destroys order, the hunger for order will destroy liberty.
    Will Durant

He that would make his own liberty secure must guard even his enemy from oppression.
    Thomas Paine

Liberty has never come from the government. Liberty has always come from the subjects of it. The history of liberty is a history of resistance. The history of liberty is a history of limitations of governmental power, not the increase of it.
    Woodrow Wilson

Let every nation know, whether it wishes us well or ill, that we shall pay any price, bear any burden, meet any hardship, support any friend, oppose any foe, in order to assure the survival and the success of liberty.
    John F. Kennedy

Civil liberties means liberties for those we like and those we don't like, or even detest.
    Felix Frankfurter

O Freedom, what liberties are taken in thy name.
    Daniel George

What is Freedom?

You cannot see it, but you will know instantly when it's gone.
You cannot feel it, but it shelters you like a robe.
You cannot taste it, but a taste was never sweeter.
You cannot hear it, but it rings out like a thousand bells.
You cannot buy it, though it often comes with a heavy cost.
You cannot sell it, for it is not yours to sell.
You cannot crush it, yet few things are more fragile.
You cannot extinguish it; the flame will rekindle.
You cannot keep it for yourself; it gathers strength when shared.
You cannot force it upon another; that is not its nature.
And while it can be stolen from someone without his or her consent, most of history's great battles have been waged to win it back.
    Senator Rod Grams - MN

O'er the land of the free, and the home of the brave!
    Francis Scott Key 1814

Who has lost his freedom has nothing else to lose.

The cost of freedom is always high, but Americans have always paid it. And one path we shall never choose, and that is the path of surrender, or submission.
    John F. Kennedy

Freedom of speech does not give a person the right to shout "Fire!" in a crowded theater.
    Oliver Wendell Holmes

We are in bondage to the law in order that we may be free.
    Cicero

Those who deny freedom to others deserve it not for themselves, and under a just God, cannot long retain it.
    Abraham Lincoln

Freedom is like a coin. It has the word privilege on one side and responsibility on the other. It does not have privilege on both sides. There are too many today who want everything involved in privilege but refuse to accept anything that approaches the sense of responsibility.
    Joseph Sizoo

When you have robbed a man of everything, he is no longer in your power. He is free again.
    Alexander Solzhenitsyn

I have a dream that one day on the red hills of Georgia the sons of former slaves and the sons of former slave owners will be able to sit down together at the table of brotherhood.
    Martin Luther King 1963

Since the general civilization of mankind I believe there are more instances of the abridgment of the freedom of the people by gradual and silent encroachments of those in power than by violent and sudden usurpations.
    James Madison

We who lived in concentration camps can remember the men who walked through the huts comforting others, giving away their last piece of bread. They may have been few in number, but they offer sufficient proof that everything can be taken from a man but one thing; the last of human freedoms - to choose one's attitude in any given set of circumstances - to choose one's own way.
    Viktor Frankl

Freedom is never free. It is always purchased at great cost.

I am well aware of the toil, and blood, and treasure, that it will cost to maintain this declaration, and support and defend these states; yet, through all the gloom I can see the rays of light and glory. I can see that the end is worth more than all the means.
    John Adams

Posterity - you will never know how much it has cost my generation to preserve your freedom. I hope you will make good use of it.
    John Quincy Adams

What we obtain too cheaply, we esteem too lightly; it is dearness only that gives everything its value. Heaven knows how to put a price upon its goods and it would be strange indeed if so celestial an article as freedom should not be highly rated.
    Thomas Payne 1776

For the support of this declaration, with a firm reliance on the protection of the Divine Providence, we mutually pledge to each other, our lives, our fortunes, and our sacred honor.
    Declaration of Independence

To be born free is a privilege. To die free is an awesome responsibility.

Our interest will be to throw open the doors of commerce, and to knock off all its shackles, giving perfect freedom to all persons for the vent of whatever they may choose to bring into our ports, and asking the same in theirs.
    Thomas Jefferson

Freedom is a breath of air,
Pine-scented, or salty like the sea;
Freedom is a field new-plowed . . .
Furrows of democracy!

Freedom is a forest,
Trees tall and straight as men!
Freedom is a printing press . . .
The power of the pen!

Freedom is a country church,
A cathedral's stately spire;
Freedom is a spirit
That can set the soul on fire!

Freedom is man's birthright,
A sacred, living rampart;
A pulse beat of humanity . . .
The throb of a nation's heart!
    Clara Smith Reber - Freedom

God who gave our fathers freedom, God who made our fathers brave, What they built with love and anguish, Let their children watch and save.
    Robert Nathan

Chapter 4

**HE WHO LOVES NOT HIS COUNTRY
CAN LOVE NOTHING.
LORD BYRON**

An American is one who loves justice and believes in the dignity of man.
    Harold L. Ickes

God send us men with hearts ablaze All truth to love, all wrong to hate; These are the patriots nations need,
    These are the bulwarks of the state.
    Frederick A. Gillman

The American dream . . . has been a dream of being able to grow to the fullest development as man and woman.
    James Truslow Adams

There has been a calculated risk in every stage of American development. The nation was built by men who took risks: pioneers who were not afraid of the wilderness, brave men who were not afraid of failure, scientists who were not afraid of truth, thinkers who were not afraid of progress, dreamers who were not afraid of action.
    Brooks Atkinson

I am an American, and therefore what I do, however small, is of importance.
    Struthers Burt

Only those Americans who are willing to die for their country are fit to live.
    Douglas MacArthur

Human history becomes more and more a race between education and catastrophe.
    H. G. Wells

We must learn to live together as brothers or perish together as fools.
    Martin Luther King - 1964

And so, my fellow American: ask not what your country can do for you - ask what you can do for your country.
    John F. Kennedy - 1961

If you once forfeit the confidence of your fellow citizens, you can never regain their respect and esteem.
    Abraham Lincoln

What men value in the world is not rights, but privileges.
    H. L. Mencken

There is no room in this country for hyphenated Americans . . . The one absolutely certain way of bringing this nation to ruin, of preventing all possibility of continuing to be a nation at all would be to permit it to become a tangle of squabbling nationalities.
    Theodore Roosevelt

I venture to suggest that patriotism is not a short and frenzied outburst of emotion but the tranquil and steady dedication of a lifetime.
    Adlai Stevenson

Patriotism is easy to understand in America; it means looking out for yourself by looking out for your country.
    Calvin Coolidge

A man who is good enough to shed his blood for his country is good enough to be given a square deal afterwards.
    Theodore Roosevelt

I am only one, but I am one. I cannot do everything, but I can do something. What I can do, I should do and, with the help of God, I will do!
    Everett Hale

Double - no triple - our troubles and we'd still be better off than any other people on earth.
    Ronald Reagan

He who loves not his country can love nothing.
    Lord Byron

The flag is many things. It is a mark of identification of ships at sea and of armies in the field. It is a means of communication. When you see our Flag in front of a home, it says for all the world to read, "Here lives a family that is American in spirit as well as in name." The Flag is a mirror, reflecting to each person his own ideals and dreams. It is a history. Its thirteen stripes and fifty stars embrace a record written greatly during these years since 1776. It is a mark of pride in a great word - the word "American." It is an aspiration of what small children want their lives to be. It is a memory at the end of life of all that life has been. It is a ribbon of honor for those who have served it well - in peace and war. It is a warning not to detour from the long road that has brought our country and its people to a degree of prosperity and happiness never even approached under any other banner.
    Edward F. Hutton

Territory is but the body of a nation. The people who inhabit its hills and valleys are its soul, its spirit, and its life.
    James A. Garfield

The true test of civilization is not the census nor the size of cities or crops, - no, but the kind of man the country turns out.
    Ralph Waldo Emerson

A man's country is not a certain area of land, of mountains, rivers and woods, - but it is a principle; and patriotism is loyalty to that principle.
    George William Curtis

Of the various executive abilities, no one excited more anxious concern than that of placing the interests of our fellow citizens in the hands of honest men, with understanding sufficient for their stations. No duty is at the same time more difficult to fulfill. The knowledge of character possessed by a single individual is of necessity limited. To seek out the best through the whole Union, we must resort to the information which from the best men, acting disinterestedly and with the purest motives, is sometimes incorrect.
    Thomas Jefferson

You cannot dedicate yourself to America unless you become in every respect and with every purpose of your will thorough Americans.
    Woodrow Wilson

I was born an American: I live as an American; I shall die an American; and I intend to perform the duties incumbent upon me in that character to the end of my career. I mean to do this with absolute disregard of personal consequences. What are the personal consequences? What is the individual man, with all the good or evil that may betide him, in comparison with the good or evil which may befall a great country, and in the midst of great transactions which concern that country's fate? Let the consequences be what they will, I am careless. No man can suffer too much, and no man can fall too soon, if he suffer, or if he fall, in the defense of the liberties and constitution of his country.
    Daniel Webster

Chapter 5

IN GOD WE TRUST

Whether God blesses America or not does not depend so much upon God as it does upon us Americans.
    C. H. Kopf

Let us not forget the religious character of our origin. Our fathers were brought here by their high veneration for the Christian religion. They journeyed by the light, and labored in its hope. They sought to incorporate its principles with the elements of their society, and to diffuse its influence through all their institutions - civil, political and literary. Let us cherish these sentiments, and extend this influence still more widely, in the full conviction that this is the happiest society, which partakes, in the highest degree of the mild and peaceable spirit of Christianity.
    Daniel Webster

Important principles may and must be inflexible.
    Abraham Lincoln

The spirit of man is more important than mere physical strength and the spiritual fiber of a nation than its wealth.
    Dwight D. Eisenhower

Remove not the ancient landmarks, which thy fathers have set.
    Proverbs 22:28

I can't tell a lie, Pa; you know I can't tell a lie. I did cut it with my hatchet.
    George Washington

The cross, and the flag are the embodiment of our ideals and teach us not only how to live but how to die.
    Douglas MacArthur

Right is right, even if everyone is against it; and wrong is wrong, even if everyone is for it.
    William Penn

I sought for the greatness and genius of America in her commodious harbors and her ample rivers, and it was not there.
I sought for the greatness and genius of America in her fertile fields and boundless forests, and it was not there. I sought for the greatness and genius of America in her rich mines and her vast world commerce, and it was not there.
I sought for the greatness and genius of America in her public school system and her institutions of learning, and it was not there.
I sought for the greatness and genius of America in her democratic congress and her matchless constitution, and it was not there. Not until I went into the churches of America and heard her pulpits flame with righteousness did I understand the secret of her genius and power.
America is great because America is good, and if America ever ceases to be good, America will cease to be great.
    Alexis de Toequeville

Our country hath a gospel of her own To preach and practice before all the world- The freedom and divinity of man, The glorious claims of human brotherhood, And the soul's fealty to none but God.
    James Russell Lowell

Without wise leadership, a nation is in trouble; but with good counselors there is safety.
    The Bible

Labor to keep alive in your breast that little spark of celestial fire called conscience.
    George Washington

Recognition of the Supreme Being is the first, the most basic, expression of Americanism. Without God, there could be no American form of government, nor American way of life.
    Dwight D. Eisenhower

A nation, which does not remember what it was yesterday, does not know what it is today, or what it is trying to do. We are trying to do a futile thing if we do not know where we came from or what we have been about.
    Woodrow Wilson

The religion, which has introduced civil liberty, is the religion of Christ and His apostles . . . to this we owe our free constitutions of government.
    Noah Webster

The first and almost the only Book deserving of universal attention is the Bible.
    John Quincy Adams

Go to the Scriptures . . . the joyful promises it contains will be a balsam to all your troubles.
    Andrew Jackson

America's Christian Origins:
The Puritans established education in the New England colonies. They gave us a thoroughgoing respect for learning, our first books, our first college, and the habit of representative government.

America's Declaration of Independence parallels themes in the Old Testament Book of Deuteronomy.

The Pilgrims, by carefully following Biblical precepts, wrote and signed the Mayflower Compact, establishing Constitutional government in America in 1620.

Sermons during the Revolutionary War frequently portrayed George Washington as America's Moses leading God's people into the Promised Land.

America's Founding Fathers, such as John Adams connected the principles of civil government with the principles of Christianity.

Prayer for the Nation
Almighty God, Who has given us this good land for our heritage, we beseech Thee that we may always prove ourselves a people mindful of Thy favor and glad to do Thy will. Bless our land with honorable industry, sound learning and pure manners.

Save us from violence, discord and confusion; from pride and arrogance and from every evil way. Defend our liberties and fashion into one united people the multitudes brought hither out of many kindreds and tongues.

Endow with the spirit of wisdom those to whom in Thy name we entrust the authority of government, that there may be justice and peace at home, and that through obedience to Thy law, we may show forth Thy praise among the nations of the earth.

In the time of prosperity, fill our hearts with thankfulness and in days of trouble, suffer not our trust in Thee to fail; all of which we ask through Jesus Christ our Lord.
    Thomas Jefferson

As mankind becomes more liberal, they will be more apt to allow, that all those who conduct themselves as worthy members of the community are equally entitled to the protection of civil government. I hope ever to see America among the foremost nations in examples of justice and liberality. And I presume, that your fellow-citizens will not forget the patriotic part which you took in the accomplishment of their revolution, and the establishment of their government; or the important assistance, which they received, from a Nation in which the Roman Catholic religion is professed . . . May the members of your Society in America, animated alone by the pure spirit of Christianity, and still conducting themselves as the faithful subjects of our free government, enjoy every temporal and spiritual felicity.
    George Washington to Roman Catholic Committee - 1790

The Washington Monument: Engraved on the metal cap on the top are the words: "Praise be to God." Lining the walls of the stairwell are such biblical phrases as "Search the Scriptures," "Holiness to the Lord," "Train up a child in the way he should go, and when he is old he will not depart from it."

The Jefferson Memorial:
God who gave us life gave us liberty. Can the liberties of a nation be secure when we have removed a conviction that these liberties are the gift of God? Indeed I tremble for my country when I reflect that God is just, that his justice cannot sleep forever.
   Thomas Jefferson

These words of Jefferson are a forceful and explicit warning that to remove God from this country will destroy it.
Senator Byrd

The Lincoln Memorial:
. . . That this Nation, under God, shall have a new birth of freedom, and that government of the people, by the people, for the people, shall not perish from the earth.

As was said 3000 years ago, so it still must be said, "The judgments of the Lord are true and righteous altogether."
   Abraham Lincoln

All the good from the Saviour of the world is communicated through this Book; but for the Book we could not know right from wrong. All the things desirable to man are contained in it.
   Abraham Lincoln

Intelligence, patriotism . . . and a firm reliance on Him who has never forsaken this favored land are still competent to adjust in the best way all our present difficulty.
   Abraham Lincoln - First Inaugural Address

It is the duty of nations, as well as men, to own their dependence upon the overruling power of God and to recognize the sublime truth announced in the Holy Scriptures and proven by all history, that those nations only are blessed whose God is the Lord.
   Abraham Lincoln

"In God we Trust," appears opposite the President of the Senate who is Vice President of the United States. The same phrase is also inscribed in the marble, backdrop to the Speaker of the House of Representatives.

Every coin minted in the United States bears, along with the bust of a past hero, these words: Liberty - In God We Trust. It was not lightly that our forefathers chose these inseparable words, for they knew the tremendous cost and sacrifice that had been paid to secure our freedom. In gratitude, they continually acknowledged that God had made and preserved our nation. They were confident that God was blessing their endeavors because they acknowledged Him and sought His aid in all their doings. They warned future generations that the day God was not earnestly revered in America, she would become a byword among nations. We would do well to review their urgent admonition and the wisdom that was theirs when they forged this great and most prosperous nation in all history.

The Supreme Court:
Above the head of the Chief Justice of the Supreme Court are the Ten Commandments, with the great American eagle protecting them.
Moses is included among the great lawgivers in Herman A. MacNeil's marble sculpture group on the east front. The crier who opens each session closes with the words, "God save the United States and the Honorable Court."

Remove not the ancient landmarks.

The Library of Congress:
Numerous quotations from Scripture are found here within its walls. One reminds each American of his responsibility to his Maker. "What doth the Lord require of thee, but to do justly and love mercy and walk humbly with thy God?" (Micah 6:8) Another quote preserves the Psalmist's acknowledgment that all nature reflects the order and beauty of the Creator. "The heavens declare the glory of God, and the firmament showeth His handiwork." (Psalm 19:1) And yet another says, "The light shineth in darkness and the darkness compreheneth it not." (John 1:5)

Our National Anthem:
The concluding words of our National Anthem summarize the fact that the United States of America was born out of a commitment to God and His principles.
"Blessed with victory and peace, may this Heav'n rescued land
Praise the Power that hath made and preserved us a nation!
Then conquer we must, when our cause it is just!'
And the star spangled banner in triumph shall wave
O'er the land of the free, and the home of the brave."
    Francis Scott Key

The moral principles and precepts contained in the Scriptures ought to form the basis of all our civil constitutions and laws. All the miseries and evils which men suffer from vice, crime, ambition, injustice, oppression, slavery, and war, proceed from their despising or neglecting the precepts contained in the Bible.
    Noah Webster

The unhealthy gap between what we preach in America and what we often practice creates a moral dry rot that eats at the very foundation of our democratic ideals and values.
    Whitney Moore Young

I have lived, Sir, a long time, and the longer I live, the more convincing proofs I see of this truth - that God governs in the affairs of men. And if a sparrow cannot fall to the ground without His notice, is it probable that an empire can rise without His aid? We have been assured, Sir, in the sacred writings, that 'except the Lord build the House they labor in vain that build it.' I firmly believe this; and I also believe that without His concurring aid we shall succeed in this political building no better than the Builders of Babel: I therefore beg leave to move - that henceforth prayers imploring the assistance of Heaven, and its blessings on our deliberations be held in this Assembly every morning before we proceed to business . . .
    Benjamin Franklin - Second Continental Congress (1775)

The foundations of our society and our government rest so much on the teachings of the Bible that it would be difficult to support them if faith in these teachings would cease to be practically universal in our country.
    Calvin Coolidge

Republican institutions in the hands of a virtuous and God-fearing nation are the very best in the world, but in the hands of a corrupt and irreligious people they are the very worst and the most effective weapons of destruction . . .
    Philip Schaff - 1888 (Church and State in the United States)

. . . our ancestors established their system of government on morality and religious sentiment. Moral habits, they believed, cannot safely be trusted on any other foundation than religious principle, nor any government be secure which is not supported by moral habits.
    Daniel Webster

The houses of lawyers are roofed with the skins of litigants.

No people can be bound to acknowledge and adore the invisible hand, which conducts the affairs of men more than the people of the United States. Every step by which they have advanced to the character of an independent nation seems to have been distinguished by some token of providential agency . . . We ought to be no less persuaded that the propitious smiles of heaven cannot be expected on a nation that disregards the eternal rules of order and right, which heaven itself has ordained.
    George Washington in his inaugural address to Congress

George Washington was responsible for the first Thanksgiving Proclamation, which reads, "Whereas it is the duty of all nations to acknowledge the providence of Almighty God, to obey his will, to be grateful for his benefits, and humbly implore His protection and favor . . ." It goes on to call the nation to thankfulness to Almighty God.
    George Washington

We find the inaugural addresses of all the Presidents, and the Constitutions of all fifty of our states, without exception, references to the Almighty God of the universe, the Author and Sustainer of our liberty.

. . . The Bible . . . is the one supreme source of revelation of the meaning of life, the nature of God and spiritual nature and need of men. It is the only guide of life, which really leads the spirit in the way of peace and salvation.
    Woodrow Wilson

We cannot diminish the value of one category of human life - the unborn - without diminishing the value of all human life . . . there is no cause more important.
    Ronald Reagan

We have been the recipients of the choicest bounties of heaven. We have been preserved, these many years, in peace and prosperity. We have grown in numbers, wealth and power, as no other nation has ever grown. But we have forgotten God. We have forgotten the gracious hand which preserved us in peace, and multiplied and enriched and strengthened us; and we have vainly imagined, in the deceitfulness of our hearts, that all these blessings were produced by some superior wisdom and virtue of our own. Intoxicated with broken success, we have become too self-sufficient to feel the necessity of redeeming and preserving grace, too proud to pray to the God that made us! It behooves us, then to humble ourselves before the offended Power, to confess our national sins, and to pray for clemency and forgiveness.
    Abraham Lincoln - April 30, 1863 Proclamation for a National Day of Fasting, Humiliation and Prayer

The choice before us is plain, Christ or chaos, conviction or compromise, discipline or disintegration. I am rather tired of hearing about our rights and privileges as American citizens. The time is come; it now is, when we ought to hear about the duties and responsibilities of our citizenship. America's future depends upon her accepting and demonstrating God's government.
    Peter Marshall

Our laws and our institutions must necessarily be based upon and embody the teachings of The Redeemer of mankind. It is impossible that it should be otherwise; and in this sense and to this extent our civilization and our institutions are emphatically Christian . . . This is a religious people. This is historically true. From the discovery of this continent to the present hour, there is a single voice making this affirmation . . . this is a Christian nation.
    Supreme Court Decision - 1892

Our Common Labor

Before all else we seek, upon our common labor as a nation, the blessings of Almighty God. And the hopes in our hearts fashion the deepest prayers of our whole people. May we pursue the right - without self-righteousness. May we know unity - without conformity. May we grow in strength - without pride in self. May we, in our dealings with all peoples of the earth, ever speak truth and serve justice. May the light of freedom, coming to all darkened lands, flame brightly - until at last the darkness is no more. May the turbulence of our age yield to a true time of peace, when men and nations share a life that honors the dignity of each, the brotherhood of all.
    Dwight D. Eisenhower

The world has forgotten, in its concern with Left, and Right, that there is an Above and Below.
    Glen Drake

To give a man full knowledge of true morality, I would send him to not other book than the New Testament.
    Locke

Let us with caution indulge the supposition that morality can be maintained without religion. Reason and experience both forbid us to expect that national morality can prevail in exclusion of religious principle.
    George Washington

If we ever pass out as a great nation, we ought to put on our tombstone: "America died of the delusion that she had moral leadership."
    Will Rogers

That's America for you. They won't let kids pray in school, but they put Bibles in prisons.

The citizens of the United States of America have a right to applaud themselves for having given to Mankind examples of an enlarged and liberal policy, a policy worthy of imitation.

. . . For happily the Government of the United States, which gives bigotry no sanction, to persecution no assistance requires only that they who live under its protection should demean themselves as good citizens, in giving it on all occasions their effectual support.

. . . I am pleased with your favorable opinion of my administration, and fervent wishes for my felicity. May the Children of the Stock of Abraham, who dwell in this land, continue to merit and enjoy the good will of the other Inhabitants, while every one shall sit in safety under his own vine and fig-tree, and there shall be none to make him afraid. May the father of all mercies scatter light and not darkness in our paths, and make us all in our several vocations useful here, and in his own due time and way everlastingly happy.
    George Washington - August 17, 1790
    To a Hebrew Congregation - Newport, Rhode Island

The Soaring Eagle is the true meaning of liberty. He mates for life and returns to the same nest every year. He takes an active role in teaching his young to fly. For thousands of years, the eagle has been admired for its grandeur, its grace in flight, and its great size and awesome power. Assisted by his powerful wings, the eagle glides effortlessly to altitudes of over 2,400 feet and is capable of using his wings to carry other eagles to safety. The eagle's keen eyesight enables him to be sensitive to approaching danger and to protect himself and his family. He displays a sense of responsibility that is a companion of genuine liberty. In so many ways the eagle illustrates the life, victory, power, and freedom that Jesus Christ came to give those who place their faith in Him. The eagle also pictures the character and qualities that made America great.

Chapter 6

**WAR IS THE LAW OF VIOLENCE,
PEACE THE LAW OF LOVE.
ANONYMOUS**

Revolutionary War Era:

Is life so dear, or peace so sweet, as to be purchased at the price of chains and slavery? Forbid it, Almighty God! I know not what course others may take; but as for me, give me liberty, or give me death!
    Patrick Henry (Virginian Patriot)

These are the times that try men's souls. The summer soldier and the sunshine patriot will, in this crisis, shrink from the service of their country, but he that stands it now, deserves the love and thanks of man and woman.
    Thomas Paine

Caesar had his Brutus - Charles the First, his Cromwell - and George the Third - Treason . . . may profit by their example. If this be treason, make the most of it.
    Patrick Henry

The period of debate is closed. Arms as the last resort must decide the contest.
    Thomas Paine

We must indeed hang together or most assuredly we shall hang separately.
    Benjamin Franklin

. . . A man's home is his castle.
    James Otis

The Redcoats are coming!
    Paul Revere

Don't fire until you see the whites of their eyes!
    William Prescott

I have not yet begun to fight!
    John Paul Jones

It is easy to be brave from a safe distance.

These United Colonies are, and of right ought to be, free and independent States.
    Richard Henry Lee (Virginian)

Fire is the test of gold, adversity of strong men!
    Seneca

It is a rough road that leads to greatness.
    Seneca

I only regret I have but one life to lose for my country.
    Nathan Hale

Tyranny like hell, is not easily conquered; yet we have this consolation with us, that the harder the conflict, the more glorious the triumph.
    Thomas Paine

I have the Honor to inform Congress, that a Reduction of the British Army . . . is most happily effected.
    George Washington

The war contributed more to enlighten the world, and diffuse a spirit of freedom and liberality among mankind, than any human event . . . that ever preceded it.
    Thomas Paine

I now take leave of you, most devoutly wishing that your latter days may be as prosperous and happy as your former ones have been glorious and honorable.
    George Washington

Let us ever remember that our interests are in concord and not in conflict, and that our true greatness rests on our victories of peace rather than those of war.

Better an egg in peace than an ox in war.
    Early American Proverb

Making peace is the most difficult work of all.

The first casualty when war comes is truth.

If you desire peace, be ever prepared for war.

We should never despair; our situation before has been unpromising and has changed for the better, so I trust, it will again.
    George Washington

I consider it as an indispensable duty to close this last act of my official life by commending the interests of our dearest country to the protection of Almighty God, and those who have the superintendence of them to his holy keeping.
    George Washington - Farewell Address 1783

There never was a good war or a bad peace.
    Benjamin Franklin

A little rebellion now and then is a good thing.
    Thomas Jefferson

Peace flourishes when reason rules.
The object of war is peace.

Great necessities call out great virtues.
    Abigail Adams - 1780

War begets no good offspring.

The feast of vultures and a waste of life are war.

War is the law of violence, peace the law of love.

Peace has won finer victories than war.

Better to keep peace than to make peace.

Peace feeds, war wastes, peace breeds, war consumes.

All is fair in love and war.

Each defeat makes us weaker for the next battle, but each conquest makes us stronger.

A sleeping fox catches no chickens.

The General ever desirous to cherish a virtuous ambition in his soldiers, as well as to foster and encourage every species of Military merit, directs that whenever any singularly meritorious action is performed, the author of it shall be permitted to wear on his facings over the left breast, the figure of a heart of purple cloth or silk, edged with narrow lace or binding. Not only instances of unusual gallantry, but also of extraordinary fidelity and essential Service in any way shall meet with a due reward . . .
Men who have merited this last distinction to be suffered to pass all guards and sentinels which officers are permitted to do.
The road to glory in a patriot army and a free country is thus open to all - this order is also to have retrospect to the earliest stages of the war, and to be considered as a permanent one.
    The Purple Heart Badge of Military Merit, established by George Washington in 1782

The Civil War Era:
Born in a log cabin, he ascended to the White House; attending school less than one year, he became a great self-taught orator and writer; beset with many defeats and disappointments, he rose above them to become one of the most revered and beloved of statesmen in all history - so reads the remarkable career of Abraham Lincoln

God bless my mother; all I am or ever hope to be I owe to her.
    Abraham Lincoln

Always bear in mind that your own resolution to succeed is more important than any other one thing.
    Abraham Lincoln

Stand with anybody that stands right. Stand with him while he is right and part with him when he goes wrong.
    Abraham Lincoln

As I would not be a slave, so I would not be a master. This expresses my idea of democracy.
    Abraham Lincoln

No man ever made such an impression in his first appeal to a New York audience.
    The New York Tribune said of Abraham Lincoln's speech at Cooper Institute in New York - 1860

The Union of these States is perpetual. No State upon its own mere motion can lawfully get out of the Union.
    Abraham Lincoln

My paramount object in this struggle is to save the Union and is not either to save or to destroy slavery.
    Abraham Lincoln

Are all the laws but one to go unexecuted and the government itself go to pieces lest that one be violated?
    Abraham Lincoln

I know that the Lord is always on the side of right. But it is my constant anxiety and prayer that I and this nation should be on the Lord's side.
    Abraham Lincoln

I claim not to have controlled events, but confess plainly that events have controlled me.
    Abraham Lincoln

A house divided against itself cannot stand. I believe this government cannot endure permanently, half slave and half free.
    Abraham Lincoln

Any kingdom divided against itself will be ruined, and a house divided against itself will fall.
    The Bible - Luke 11:17 (NIV)

In giving freedom to the slave, we assure freedom to the free - honourable alike in what we give and what we preserve.
    Abraham Lincoln

Here I have lived a quarter of a century, and have passed from a young man to an old man. Here my children have been born and one is buried. I now leave not knowing when or whether ever, I may return, with a task before me greater than that which rested upon Washington. Without the assistance of that Divine Being who ever attended him, I cannot succeed. With that assistance, I cannot fail.
    Abraham Lincoln - Farewell Address in Springfield, Illinois on becoming the 16th President in 1861

The country has placed me at the helm of the ship; I'll try to steer her through.
    Abraham Lincoln

So you're the little woman who wrote the book that made this great war!
    Abraham Lincoln - on meeting Harriet Beecher Stowe author of Uncle Tom's Cabin

If my name ever gets into history, it will be for this act, and my whole soul is in it.
    Abraham Lincoln upon signing the Emancipation Proclamation - freeing the slaves

The Father of Waters again goes unvexed to the sea.
    Abraham Lincoln - when General Grant won at Vicksburg, Mississippi

Fourscore-and-seven years ago our fathers brought forth on this continent a new nation, conceived in liberty and dedicated to the proposition that all men are created equal. Now we are engaged in a great civil war, testing whether that nation or any nation so conceived and so dedicated can long endure. We are met on a great battle-field of that war. We have come to dedicate a portion of that field, as a final resting place for those who here gave their lives that that nation might live. . .
    Abraham Lincoln - Gettysburg Address

Wars bring scars.
    Clarke

With the fearful strain that is on me night and day, if I did not laugh I should die.
    Abraham Lincoln

Were it not for my little jokes, I could not bear the burdens of this office.
    Abraham Lincoln

I told God that I had done all that I could and that now the result was in His hands; that if this country was to be saved, it was because He so willed it!
The burden rolled off my shoulders. My intense anxiety was relieved and in its place came a great trustfulness!
    Abraham Lincoln

If we do not make a common cause to save the good old ship of the Union on this voyage, nobody will have a chance to pilot her on another voyage.
    Abraham Lincoln

I don't know who my grandfather was; I am much more concerned to know what his grandson will be.
    Abraham Lincoln

It is the face of a brave and noble man.
    Abraham Lincoln said of a picture of General Robert E. Lee

To give victory to the right, not bloody bullets, but peaceful ballots only are necessary.
    Abraham Lincoln

The probability that we may fail in the struggle ought not to deter us from the support of a cause we believe to be just.
    Abraham Lincoln

Fondly do we hope - fervently do we pray - that this mighty scourge of war may speedily pass away . . . With malice toward none; with charity for all; with firmness in the right, as God gives us to see the right, let us strive on to finish the work we are in; to bind up the nation's wounds; to care for him who shall have borne the battle, and for his widow, and his orphan - to do all which may achieve and cherish a just and lasting peace among ourselves, and with all nations.
    Abraham Lincoln - Second Inaugural Address - March 4, 1865

There is a true glory and a true honor, the glory of duty done, the honor of the integrity of principle.
    Robert E. Lee

Virginia is my country; her I will obey, however lamentable the fate to which it may subject me.
    Robert E. Lee

While I wish to do what is right, I am unwilling to do what is wrong, either at the bidding of the South or of the North.
    Robert E. Lee

God alone can save us from our folly, selfishness, and shortsightedness . . . I am unable to realize that our people will destroy a government inaugerated by the blood and wisdom of our patriot fathers. . . I wish to live under no other government.
    Robert E. Lee

There was not a man in the Confederacy whose influence with the whole people was as great as his.
    Ulysses S. Grant said of Robert E. Lee

Success in Mexico was largely due to the skill, valor, and undaunted courage of Robert E. Lee . . . the greatest military genius in America.
    General Winfield Scott said of Lee during the Mexican War

It is well that war is so terrible - we would grow too fond of it.
    Robert E. Lee - during the Battle of Fredericksburg - 1862

Then there is nothing left me but to go and see General Grant, and I would rather die a thousand deaths.
    Robert E. Lee contemplating surrender of the Confederate Army

Men, we have fought through the war together. I have done my best for you; my heart is too full to say more.
    Robert E. Lee - just before he surrendered to Ulysses S. Grant

After four years of arduous service, marked by unsurpassed courage and fortitude, the Army of Northern Virginia has been compelled to yield to overwhelming numbers and resources. I need not tell the survivors of so many hard-fought battles, who have remained steadfast to the last, that I have consented to this result from no distrust of them; but, feeling that valour and devotion could accomplish nothing . . .
I have determined to avoid the useless sacrifice of those whose past services have endeared them to their countrymen. . . . I bid you an affectionate farewell.
    General Robert E. Lee

No terms except an unconditional and immediate surrender can be accepted.
    Ulysses S. Grant - when he lay siege to Fort Donelson - thus his nickname Unconditional Surrender Grant

War is Hell!
    William Tecumseh Sherman - on his march through Georgia from Atlanta to the sea, destroying the South's economic resources

There is many a boy here today who looks on war as all glory, but boys, it is all hell.
    General Sherman

Tell a man he is brave, and you help him to become so.
    Thomas Carlyle

A Great War leaves the country with three armies: an army of cripples, an army of mourners, and an army of thieves.

In wars, laws have no authority.

War hath no fury like a non-combatant.
    C. E. Montague

The war is over; the rebels are our countrymen again.
    General Grant

I have fought against the people of the North because I believed they were seeking to wrest from the South dearest rights. But I have never cherished bitter or vindictive feelings, and have never seen a day when I did not pray for them.
    Robert E. Lee

Now he belongs to the ages.
    Secretary of War - Stanton said just after the death of President Lincoln

It is by no means necessary that a great nation should always stand at the heroic level. But no nation has the root of greatness in it unless in time of need it can rise to the heroic level.
    Theodore Roosevelt

Far better it is to dare mighty things, to win glorious triumphs, even though checkered by failure, than to take rank with those poor spirits who neither enjoy much nor suffer much, because they live in the gray twilight that knows not victory or defeat.
    Theodore Roosevelt

Peace is goodwill in action.

There is only one step from the sublime to the ridiculous.
    Napoleon Bonaparte

Take time to deliberate, but when the time for action has arrived, stop thinking and go in.
    Napoleon Bonaparte

Never awake me when you have good news to announce, because with good news nothing presses; but when you have bad news, arouse me immediately, for then there is not an instant to be lost.
    Napoleon Bonaparte

An army marches on its stomach.
    Napoleon Bonaparte

Politics is war without bloodshed while war is politics with bloodshed.
    Mao Tse-tung

After each war there is a little less democracy to save.
Four things greater than all things are:
Women, and Horses, and Power and War.
    Rudyard Kipling

Those who cannot remember the past are condemned to repeat it.

When the going gets tough, the tough get going.
    Joseph P. Kennedy

Face the conflict. To run from it will be a continual race.
    R. E. Phillips

Conflict can be an opportunity for growth or the tool for destruction of relationships.

This will remain the land of the free only so long as it is the home of the brave.
    Elmer Davis

The test of tolerance comes when we are in a majority; the test of courage comes when we are in a minority.
    Ralph W. Sockman

In the heart of the fearless, there is nothing but victory. Cowards die a thousand deaths, Brave men only one.

Man's inhumanity to man makes countless thousands mourn.

Great victories come, not through ease but by fighting valiantly and meeting hardships bravely.

Consider wherein you agree with your opponent rather than wherein you differ.

O Freedom, what liberties are taken in thy name.

    World War Era:
Courage is the first of human qualities because it is the quality, which guarantees all the others.
    Winston Churchill

The only thing we have to fear is fear itself.
    Franklin D. Roosevelt

Bravery is the capacity to perform properly even when scared half to death.
    General Omar Bradley

Yesterday, December 7, 1941 - a date which will live in infamy - the United States of America was suddenly and deliberately attacked by naval and air forces of the Empire of Japan.
    Franklin D. Roosevelt - 1941

In War: Resolution. In Defeat: Defiance.
In Victory: Magnanimity. In Peace: Goodwill.
    Winston Churchill

I want you.
    Uncle Sam

Inferiors revolt in order that they may be equal, and equals that they may be superior.
    Aristotle

What better fate for a man than to die in the performance of his duty?
    Douglas MacArthur

Justice without force is powerless; force without justice is tyrannical.
    Blaise Pascal

A man convinced against his will is of the same opinion still.
    Samuel Butler

In the last 3,421 years of recorded history, only 268 have seen no war.
    Ariel and Will Durant

I don't know what kinds of weapons will be used in the third world war; assuming there will be a third world war. But I can tell you what the fourth world war will be fought with - stone clubs.
Albert Einstein Loose lips, sink ships.
The one means that wins the easiest victory over reason: terror and force.
    Adolf Hitler

Lafayette, We Are Here!
    General John J. Pershing landed in
    France - 1917

The world must be made safe for democracy.
    Woodrow Wilson - 1917

History teaches us that man never learns from history, therefore, he is apt to repeat it.

          Leadership:
You must have clear goals for the mission.
Give yourself a clear agenda for the day.
Let people know where they stand. What's broken, fix now. Don't put it off.
No repainting the flagpole. Make sure all the work you require is essential.
Set high standards. People generally won't perform above your expectations.
Lay the concept out, but let your people execute it. Allow them to own their work.
People come to work to succeed not to fail.
Never lie, ever.
When in charge, take command. Do what's right.
    General H. Norman Schwarzkoff

Chapter 7

WE THE PEOPLE OF THE UNITED STATES, IN ORDER TO FORM A MORE PERFECT UNION, ESTABLISH JUSTICE, INSURE DOMESTIC TRANQUILITY, PROVIDE FOR THE COMMON DEFENSE, PROMOTE THE GENERAL WELFARE, AND SECURE THE BLESSINGS OF LIBERTY TO OURSELVES AND OUR POSTERITY, DO ORDAIN AND ESTABLISH THIS CONSTITUTION FOR THE UNITED STATES OF AMERICA. THE PREAMBLE TO THE CONSTITUTION

THOMAS JEFFERSON

Plymouth Rock Inscription:
This spot marks the final resting-place of the Pilgrims of the Mayflower. In weariness and hunger and in cold,
fighting the wilderness and burying their dead in common graves that the Indians should not know how many had perished, they here laid the foundations of a state in which all men for countless ages should have liberty to worship God in their own way. All ye who pass by and see this stone remember, and dedicate yourselves anew to the resolution that you will not rest until this lofty ideal shall have been realized throughout the earth.

The Mayflower Compact,
November 11, 1620
In the Name of God, Amen. We, whose names are underwritten, the Loyal Subjects of our dread Sovereign Lord King James, by the Grace of God, of Great Britain, France, and Ireland, King, Defender of the Faith, etc. Having undertaken for the Glory of God, and Advancement of the Christian Faith, and the Honour of our King and Country, a Voyage to plant the first Colony in the northern Parts of Virginia; Do by these Presents, solemnly and mutually, in the Presence of God and one another, covenant and combine ourselves together into a civil Body Politick, for our better Ordering and Preservation, and Furtherance of the Ends aforesaid: And by Virtue hereof do enact, constitute, and frame, such just and equal Laws, Ordinances, Acts, Constitutions, and Officers, from time to time, as shall be thought most meet and convenient for the general Good of the Colony; unto which we promise all due Submission and Obedience. In Witness whereof we have hereunto subscribed our names at Cape-Cod the eleventh of November, in the Reign of our Sovereign Lord King James, of England, France, and Ireland, the eighteenth, and of Scotland, the fifty- fourth, Anno Domini, 1620.
 (To which forty-one signatures were added)

The Unanimous Declaration of the Thirteen United States of America -
July 4, 1776
When in the Course of human events, it becomes necessary for one people to dissolve the political bands which have connected them with another, and to assume among the powers of the earth, the separate and equal station to which the Laws of Nature and of Nature's God entitle them, a decent respect to the opinions of mankind requires that they should declare the causes which impel them to the separation.
We hold these truths to be self-evident, that all men are created equal, that they are endowed by their Creator with certain unalienable Rights, that among these are Life, Liberty, and the pursuit of Happiness. . . . That to secure these rights, Governments are instituted among Men, deriving their just powers from the consent of the governed. . . . We, Therefore, the Representatives of the United States of America, in General Congress, Assembled, appealing to the Supreme Judge of the world for the rectitude of our intentions, do, in the Name, and by Authority of the good People of these Colonies, solemnly publish and declare, That these United Colonies are, and of Right ought to be, Free And Independent States; that they are Absolved from All Allegiance to the British Crown, and that all political connection between them and the State of Great Britain, is and ought to be totally dissolved; and that as Free and Independent States, they have full Power to levy War, conclude Peace, contract Alliances, establish Commerce, and to do all other Acts and Things which Independent States may of right do. And for the support of this Declaration, with a firm reliance on the protection of Divine Providence, we mutually pledge to each other our Lives, our Fortunes, and our sacred Honor.
 (To which 56 men signed their names - One, John Hancock, signed it large enough so King George could read it without his spectacles on.)

The Preamble to the Constitution

We the People of the United States, in order to form a more perfect Union, establish Justice, insure domestic Tranquility, provide for the common Defense, promote the general Welfare, and secure the Blessings of Liberty to ourselves and our Posterity, do ordain and establish this Constitution for the United States of America.

The American's Creed By William Tyler Page Adopted on April 3, 1918

I believe in the United States of America as a government of the people, by the people, for the people: whose just powers are derived from the consent of the governed; a democracy in a Republic; a sovereign Nation of many sovereign States; a perfect Union, one and inseparable; established upon those principles of freedom, equality, justice and humanity for which American patriots sacrificed their lives and fortunes.
I therefore believe it is my duty to my Country to love it; to support its Constitution; to obey its laws; to respect its flag, and to defend it against all enemies.

The New Colossus
By Emma Lazarus
(The Statue of Liberty
Sculptor - Auguste Bartholdi)

Not like the brazen giant of Greek fame, With conquering limbs astride from land to land; Here at our sea-washed, sunset gates shall stand A mighty woman with a torch, whose flame Is the imprisoned lightning, and her name Mother of Exiles. From her beacon-hand Glows world wide welcome; her mild eyes command The air-bridged harbor that twin cities frame. "Keep ancient lands, your storied pomp!" cries she with silent lips. "Give me your tired, your poor, your huddled masses yearning to breathe free. The wretched refuse of your teeming shore. Send these, the homeless, tempest-tost to me. I lift my lamp beside the golden door!"

A Call To Arms - under General George Washington

To all brave, healthy, able bodied, and well disposed young men, in this neighborhood, who have any inclination to join the troops, now raising under General Washington, for the defense of the Liberties And Independence of the United States, against the hostile designs of foreign enemies, Take Notice, . . . The Encouragement at this time, to enlist, is truly liberal and generous, namely, a bounty of Twelve dollars, an annual and fully sufficient supply of good and handsome clothing, a daily allowance of a large and ample ration of provisions, together with Sixty dollars a year in Gold and Silver money on account of pay, the whole of which the soldier may lay up for himself and friends, as all articles proper for his substance and comfort are provided by law, without any expense to him.
Those who may favor this recruiting party with their attendance as above, will have an opportunity of hearing and seeing in a more particular manner, the great advantages which these brave men will have, who shall embrace this opportunity of spending a few happy years in viewing the different parts of this beautiful continent, in the honorable and truly respectable character of a soldier, after which, he may, if he pleases return home to his friends, with his pockets Full of money and his head covered with laurels.
God Save the United States.

The Pledge of Allegiance

I pledge allegiance to the flag of the United States of America and to the Republic for which it stands, one Nation under God, indivisible, with Liberty and Justice for all. (Such pledge should be rendered by standing with the right hand over the heart. However, civilians will always show full respect to the flag when the pledge is given by merely standing at attention, men removing their headdress. Persons in uniform shall render the military salute.)

The Bill of Rights

Article 1
Congress shall make no law respecting an establishment of religion, or prohibiting the free exercise thereof; or abridging the freedom of speech or of the press; or the right of the people peaceably to assemble and to petition the Government for a redress of grievances.

Article 2
A well-regulated militia being necessary to the security of a free State, the right of the people to keep and bear arms shall not be infringed.

Article 3
No soldier shall, in time of peace, be quartered in any house without the consent of the owner, nor in time of war but in a manner to be prescribed by law.

Article 4
The right of the people to be secure in their persons, houses, papers, and effects, against unreasonable searches and seizures, shall not be violated, and no warrants shall issue but upon probable cause, supported by oath or affirmation, and particularly describing the place to be searched, and the persons or things to be seized.

Article 5
No person shall be held to answer for a capital or other infamous crime unless on a presentment or indictment of a Grand Jury, except in cases arising in the land or naval forces, or in the militia, when in actual service, in time of war or public danger; nor shall any person be subject for the same offense to be twice put in jeopardy of life or limb; nor shall be compelled in any criminal case to be a witness against himself, nor be deprived of life, liberty, or property, without due process of law; nor shall private property be taken for public use without just compensation.

Article 6
In all criminal prosecutions, the accused shall enjoy the right to a speedy and public trial, by an impartial jury of the State and district wherein the crime shall have been committed, which districts shall have been previously ascertained by law, and to be informed of the nature and cause of the accusation; to be confronted with the witnesses against him; to have compulsory process for obtaining witnesses in his favor, and to have the assistance of counsel for his defense.

Article 7
In suits at common law, where the value in controversy shall exceed twenty dollars, the right of trial by jury shall be preserved, and no fact tried by a jury shall be otherwise re-examined in any court of the United States than according to the rules of the common law.

Article 8
Excessive bail shall not be required, nor excessive fines imposed, nor cruel and unusual punishments inflicted.

Article 9
The enumeration in the Constitution of certain rights shall not be construed to deny or disparage others retained by the people.

Article 10
The powers not delegated to the United States by the Constitution, nor prohibited by it to the States, are reserved to the States, respectively, or to the people.

Hail Columbia
The President's March to honor President Washington - 1798
Verses 1 & 4

Hail, Columbia, happy land! Hail ye heroes! heav'n-born band! Who fought and bled in Freedom's cause, Who
fought and bled in Freedom's cause, And when the storm of war was gone, Enjoyed the peace your valor won. Let independence be our boast, Ever mindful what it cost; Ever grateful for the prize, Let its altar reach the skies. Firm, united, let us be, Rallying around our liberty; As a band of brothers joined, Peace and safety we shall find.
Behold the Chief who now commands, Once more to serve his country stands, The rock on which the storm will beat, The rock on which the storm will beat; But armed in virtue, firm and true, His hopes are fixed on heav'n and you.
When hope was sinking in dismay, When gloom obscured Columbia's Day, His steady mind, from changes free, Resolved on death or liberty.

The Gettysburg Address
By Abraham Lincoln
November 19, 1863

Fourscore and seven years ago our fathers brought forth on this continent a new nation conceived in liberty and dedicated to the proposition that all men are created equal. Now we are engaged in a great civil war, testing whether that nation or any nation so conceived and so dedicated, can long endure. We are met on a great battlefield of that war. We have come to dedicate a portion of that field, as a final resting-place for those who here gave their lives that that nation might live. It is altogether fitting and proper that we should do this.

But, in a larger sense, we can not dedicate - we can not consecrate - we can not hallow - this ground. The brave men, living and dead, who struggled here, have consecrated it, far above our poor power to add or detract. The world will little note, nor long remember what we say here, but it can never forget what they did here. It is for us the living, rather, to be dedicated here to the unfinished work, which they who

fought here thus far so nobly advanced. It is rather for us to be here dedicated to the great task remaining before us - that from these honored dead we take increased devotion to that cause for which they gave the last full measure of devotion - that we here highly resolve that these dead shall not have died in vain - that this nation, under God, shall have a new birth of freedom - and that government of the people, by the people, for the people, shall not perish from the earth.

Yankee Doodle

Father and I went down to camp, A-long with Captain Gooding, And there we see the men and boys As thick as hasty pudding.
Yankee Doodle keep it up, Yankee Doodle dandy, Mind the music and the steps, And with the girls be handy.
And there we see a thousand men, As rich as 'squire- David, And what they wasted ev'ry day, I wish it had been saved.

Dixie
By Daniel D. Emmett

I wish I was in de land ob cotton, Old times dar am not forgotten, Look away! Look away! Look away! Dixie Land. In Dixie Land whar I was born in, - Early on one frosty mornin', Look away! Look away! Look away! Dixie Land.
Chorus:
Den I wish I was in Dixie, Hooray! Hooray! In Dixie Land, I'll take my stand To lib and die in Dixie, Away, Away, Away down south in Dixie, Away, Away, Away down south in Dixie.

Tenting on the Old Camp Ground
By Walter Kittredge

We're tenting tonight on the old camp ground, Give us a song to cheer our weary hearts, a song of home, And friends we love so dear,
Chorus:
Many are the hearts that are weary tonight, Wishing for the war to cease; Many are the hearts looking for the right, To see the dawn of peace.
Tenting tonight, Tenting tonight, tenting on the old camp ground.
We've been tenting tonight on the old camp ground, Thinking of days gone by, Of the loved ones at home that gave us the hand, And the tear that said "good- bye!"

The Battle Hymn of the Republic
By Julia Ward Howe

Mine eyes have seen the glory of the coming of the Lord; He is trampling out the vintage where the grapes of wrath are stored; He hath loosed the fateful lightning of His terrible swift sword, His truth is marching on.
Chorus:
Glory! Glory! Hallelujah! Glory! Glory! Hallelujah! Glory! Glory! Hallelujah! His truth is marching on.
I have seen Him in the watch fires of a hundred circling camps; They have builded Him an altar in the evening dews and damps; I can read His righteous sentence by the dim and flaring lamps, His day is marching on.

The Star-Spangled Banner
By Francis Scott Key - 1814
(It became America's National Anthem by an act of Congress in 1931.)

O! say, can you see, by the dawn's early light, What so proudly we hailed at the twilight's last gleaming: Whose broad stripes and bright stars through the perilous fight, O'er the ramparts we watched were so gallantly streaming, And the rocket's red glare, the bombs bursting in air, Gave proof through the night that our flag was still there;

Chorus:
O! say, does that Star-spangled Banner still wave O'er the land of the free and the home of the brave?

O! thus be it ever when free men shall stand Between their loved homes and the foe's desolation; Bless'd with victory and peace, may our Heaven-rescued land Praise the Power that hath made and preserved us a nation. Then conquer we must, when our cause it is just, And this be our motto - "In God is our trust!"

Chorus:
And the Star-spangled Banner in triumph shall wave O'er the land of the free and the home of the brave.

America
By Rev. Samuel F. Smith

My country 'tis of thee, Sweet land of liberty, Of thee I sing; Land where my fathers died; Land of the pilgrim's pride; From ev'ry mountain side Let freedom ring.

My native country, thee, Land of the noble free, Thy name I love; I love thy rocks and rills, Thy woods and templed hills; My heart with rapture thrills, Like that above.

Let music swell the breeze, And ring from all the trees Sweet freedom's song; Let mortal tongues awake, Let all that breathe partake; Let rocks their silence break, The sound prolong.

Our father's God! to thee, Author of liberty, To Thee we sing; Long may our land be bright With freedom's holy light; Protect us by Thy might, Great God our King.

America the Beautiful
By Katharine Lee Bates
(Inspiration from Pike's Peak - 1893)

O beautiful for spacious skies, For amber waves of grain, For purple mountains majesties Above the fruited plain! America! America! God shed His grace on thee - And crown thy good with brotherhood From sea to shining sea!

O beautiful for pilgrim feet, Whose stern, impassion'd stress, - A thoroughfare for freedom beat Across the wilderness: America! America! God mend thine ev'ry flaw, Confirm thy soul in self-control, Thy liberty in law! O beautiful for heroes proved In liberating strife, - Who more than self their country loved, And mercy more than life! America! America! May God thy gold refine - Till all success be nobleness And every gain divine!

O beautiful for patriot dream That sees beyond the years Thine alabaster cities gleam Undimmed by human tears! America! America! God shed His grace on thee - And crown thy good with brotherhood From sea to shining sea!

Credo
By Wendell L. Wilkie

I believe in America because in it we are free - free to choose our government, to speak our minds, to observe our different religions; Because we are generous with our freedom - we share our rights with those who disagree with us; Because we hate no people and covet no people's land; Because we are blessed with a natural and varied abundance; Because we set no limit to a man's achievement: in mine, factory, field, or service in business or the arts, an able man, regardless of class or creed, can realize his ambition; Because we have great dreams - and because we have the opportunity to make those dreams come true.

PART THREE

EARTH'S WONDERS AND RESOURCES

COME FORTH INTO THE LIGHT OF THINGS,
LET NATURE BE YOUR TEACHER, SHE HAS
A WORLD OF READY WEALTH ...
WILLIAM WORDSWORTH

Chapter 1

**ANIMALS CAN SOMETIMES WARM YOUR
HEART BETTER THAN PEOPLE CAN.
ANONYMOUS**

In every living creature is the spirit to be free.

Whatever happens to the beasts also happens to man.
    Chief Seattle

I wish the bald eagle had not been chosen as the representative of our country . . . the turkey is a much more respectable bird, and withal a true original native of America.
    Benjamin Franklin

Not the cry, but the flight of the wild duck, leads the flock to fly and follow.
    Chinese Proverb

Animals can sometimes warm your heart better than people can.

The first time you attempt to feed a wild animal, it will run away.

If an animal does something they call it instinct. If we do exactly the same thing for the same reason, they call it intelligence. I guess what they mean is that we all make mistakes, but intelligence enables us to do it on purpose.
    Will Cuppy

An animal's eyes have the power to speak a great language.
    Martin Buber

Animals are such agreeable friends - they ask no questions, they pass no criticisms.
    George Eliot

Behold the turtle. He makes progress only when he sticks his neck out.
    James B. Conant

Consider the little mouse, how sagacious an animal it is which never entrusts its life to one hole only.
    Titus Maccius Plautus

The bird a nest, the spider a web, man friendship.
    William Blake

Dogs laugh, but they laugh with their tails.
    Max Eastman

What matters is not the size of the dog in the fight, but the size of the fight in the dog.
    Coach Bear Bryant

"Just living is not enough," said the butterfly. "One must have sunshine, freedom, and a little flower."
    Hans Christian Andersen

Happiness is like a butterfly.
The more you chase it, the more it will elude you; But if you turn your attention to other things, It comes and softly sits on your shoulder.
    L. Richard Lessor

The butterfly counts not months but moments and yet has time enough.

It is easy to dodge an elephant but not a fly.

    The Elephant
When people call this beast to mind, They marvel more and more
At such a little tail behind, So large a trunk before.
    Hilaire Belloc

Birds are the 'early warning system' of man's damage to the environment.
    Roger Tory Peterson

The giraffe, in their queer, inimitable, vegetative gracefulness, as if it were not a herd of animals but a family of rare, long-stemmed, speckled, gigantic flowers slowly advancing.
    Karen Blixen

The Pedigree of honey Does not concern the Bee - A clover, any time, to him, Is aristocracy -
    Emily Dickinson

Chapter 2

HURT NOT THE EARTH, NEITHER THE SEA,
NOR THE TREES.
THE BIBLE - REVELATION 7:3

Hurt not the earth, neither the sea, nor the trees.
    The Bible - Revelations 7:3

Sell the country? Why not sell the air, the clouds and the great sea, as well as the earth? Did not the Great Spirit make them all for the use of his children?
    Shawnee Chief Tecumseh - in response to General Washington's proposal to buy Indian lands.

When we see land as a community to which we belong, we may begin to use it with love and respect.
    Aldo Leopold

The foolish man seeks happiness in the distance; the wise grows it under his feet.
    James Oppenheim

Without heat and pressure, there would be no diamonds. Tough situations provide opportunities to shine.

A diamond is a chunk of coal that made good under pressure.

I am a passenger on the spaceship earth.
    Gerard Manley Hopkins

The face and character of our country are determined by what we do with America and its resources.
    Thomas Jefferson

A lake is the landscape's most beautiful and expressive feature. It is earth's eye, looking into which the beholder measures the depth of his own nature.
    Henry David Thoreau

Like water which can clearly mirror the sky and the trees only so long as its surface is undisturbed, the mind can only reflect the true image of the Self when it is tranquil and wholly relaxed.
    Indra Devi

I have no father but the sun - no mother but the earth. She feeds me, she clothes me, and I shall recline upon her bosom.
    Chief Pontiac

Earth provides enough to satisfy every man's needs, but not every man's greed.
    Mohandas K. Gandhi

We have not inherited the earth from our fathers; we are borrowing it from our children.
    Native American Saying

Conservation is a state of harmony between men and land.
    Aldo Leopold

A small rock holds back a great wave.
    Homer

To everything there is a season, and a time to every purpose under heaven.
    The Bible - Ecclesiastes 3:1

Climb the mountains and get their good tidings. Nature's peace will flow into you as sunshine flows into trees. The winds will flow their own freshness into you and the storms their energy, while cares will drop off like autumn leaves.
    John Muir

In the mountains, we forget to count the days.
    Japanese Proverb

Chapter 3

**WE CAN NEVER HAVE ENOUGH OF NATURE.
HENRY DAVID THOREAU**

We should all be concerned about the future because we will have to spend the rest of our lives there.
    Charles F. Kettering

Men of ill judgment oft ignore the good that lies within their hands, till they have lost it.
    Sophocles

There is no trifling with Nature; it is always in the right . . .
    Johann Wolfgang Von Goethe

There is something infinitely healing in the repeated refrains of nature.
    Rachel Carson

Every man's life is a fairytale written by God's fingers.
    Hans Christian Andersen

If the path be beautiful, let us not ask where it leads.
    Anatole France

Though we travel the world over to find the beautiful, we must carry it with us or we find it not.
    Ralph Waldo Emerson

Variety of uniformities makes complete beauty.
    Sir Christopher Wren

Every day is a new beginning; every morn is the world made new.

We can never have enough of nature.
    Henry David Thoreau

We own nothing. We are merely the keepers and caretakers of everything we have.

Take time to enjoy and appreciate the beauty of nature.

If you find a path with no obstacles, it probably doesn't lead anywhere.

Seek the promise of the future in the lessons of the past.

Teach your senses to perceive the beauty in all things.

Beauty can be found in art, music, nature, a person's face or soul, and anything else that gives one pleasure.

Nature never did betray the heart that loved her.
    Seneca

One touch of nature makes the whole world kin.
    William Shakespeare

Everything has a purpose. Even the cataclysmic destruction of a forest fire clears the path for rebirth.

I love to think of nature as an unlimited broadcast station, through which God speaks to us every hour, if only we will listen.
    George Washington Carver

Plans to protect air and water, wilderness and wildlife are in fact plans to protect man.
    Stewart Udall

Come forth into the light of things; let nature be your teacher, she has a world of ready wealth . . .
    William Wordsworth

Perhaps nature is our best assurance of immortality.
   Eleanor Roosevelt

Stop and consider! Life is but a day; a fragile dew drop on its perilous way from a tree's summit.
   John Keats

It is the simple things that make living worthwhile, the sweet fundamental things such as love and duty, work and rest and living close to nature.
   Laura Ingalls Wilder

Nature is often hidden, sometimes overcome, seldom extinguished.
   Francis Bacon

Nature has an etiquette all her own.
   Ludwig Van Beethoven

Use it up, wear it out, make it do, or do without.
   New England Proverb

There is a pleasure in the pathless woods, There is a rapture on the lonely shore, There is a society where none intrudes, By the deep sea, and music in its roar: I love not man the less, but nature more.
   Lord Byron

Something deep in our spirit makes us long to be out of doors, to be renewed in the presence of nature. If you listen, the world of sky and water and trees can teach you. It can change you. It can make your life profoundly simpler and more satisfying.
   Thomas Kinkade

There is no other door to knowledge than the door Nature opens; and there is no truth except the truths we discover in Nature.
   Luther Burbank

Some people think that as soon as you plant a tree, it must bear fruit. We must allow it to grow a bit.
   Prince Tunku Putra

The goal of life is living in agreement with nature.
   Zeno of Citium

Colors speak all languages.

Nothing is more beautiful than the loveliness of the woods before sunrise.
   George Washington Carver

Chapter 4

**AMONG MY FLOWERS AND TREES. . .
I BREATHE FREELY AS THE FIRST MAN.
ALEXANDER SMITH**

In the woods, I feel that nothing can befall me in life - no disgrace, no calamity which nature cannot repair.
    Emerson

Nothing is more beautiful than the loveliness of the woods before sunrise.
    George Washington Carver

The Admiral (Columbus) says that he never beheld so fair a thing; trees all along the river, beautiful and green, and different from ours, with flowers and fruits each according to their kind, many birds and little birds which sang very sweetly.
    Christopher Columbus' journal - 1st voyage, 1492

Of all the trees that grow so fair Old England to adorn, Greater are none beneath the Sun, Than oak, and ash, and thorn.
    Rudyard Kipling

I think that I shall never see A billboard lovely as a tree. Indeed, unless the billboards fall, I'll never see a tree at all.
    Ogden Nash

He who plants trees loves others besides himself.
    Thomas Fuller

Among my flowers and trees . . . I breathe freely as the first man.
    Alexander Smith

Growth is the only evidence of life.

A tree will not only lie as it falls, but it will fall as it leans.

The greatest trees are humble enough to bend in the wind. To avoid any suffering is like resisting the wind.

Good timber does not grow in ease, The stronger wind, the stronger trees; The farther sky the greater length, The more the storms the more the strength.
By sun and cold, by rain and snow, In tree or man good timber grows.

When you come across a tree that you do not recognize, learn its name before you consider chopping it down.

That which grows fast withers as rapidly; that which grows slowly endures.
    Josiah Gilbert Holland

With time and patience the mulberry leaf becomes a silk gown.
    Chinese Proverb

Even if I knew certainly the world would end tomorrow, I would plant an apple tree today.
    Martin Luther

Remove nothing from the forest except: nourishment for the soul, consolation for the heart, inspiration for the mind.
    Forest Plaque

Tall oaks from little acorns grow.
    David Everett

A tree is a God created solar powered air conditioner.
    Walter Barrows

I never before knew the full value of trees. Under them I breakfast, dine, write, read and receive my company.
    Thomas Jefferson

Use what talents you have; the woods would have little music if no birds sang their song except those who sang best.
    Oliver G. Wilson

A tree saved is a tree grown.
    Calvin Coolidge

Things bygone are the only things that last: The present is mere grass, quick- mown away; The past is stone, and stands forever fast.
    Eugene Lee Hamilton

I will be the gladdest thing under the sun; I will touch a hundred flowers and not pick one.
    Edna St. Vincent Millay

Gather ye rosebuds while ye may, old time is still a-flying; and this same flower that smiles today, tomorrow will be dying.
    Robert Herrick

Be no more by a storm dismayed, For by it the full-grown seeds are laid; And though the tree by its might it shatters, What then, if thousands of seeds it scatters?

Flowers are words, which even a babe may understand.
    Bishop Coxe

With a few flowers in my garden, half a dozen pictures and some books, I live without envy.
    Lope de Vega

When the sun of fortune smiles, 'tis like a harvest day, we should be busy when the corn is ripe.
    Goethe

A seed is a potential flower.

And in the woods a fragrance rare Of wild azaleas fills the air,
And richly tangled overhead
We see their blossoms sweet and red.
    Dora Read Goodale

All the flowers of all the tomorrows are in the seeds of today.

Arranging a bowl of flowers in the morning can give a sense of quiet in a crowded day - like writing a poem, or saying a prayer.
    Anne Morrow Lindbergh

Every flower of the field, every fiber of a plant, every particle of an insect, carries with it the impress of its Master and can
- if duly considered - read us lectures of ethics or divinity.
    Thomas Pope Blunt

As the blossom cannot tell what becomes of its fragrance, so no one can tell what becomes of his influence.

What is a weed? A plant whose virtues have not yet been discovered.
    Ralph Waldo Emerson

The best flower won't grow in the worst dirt, but the poorest flower will thrive in the richest loam.

Roses have thorns. They are never a surprise, so therefore, rarely a problem.

The flower that follows the sun does so even on cloudy days.

We must cultivate our garden.
    Voltaire

Green fingers are the extensions of a verdant heart.
    Russell Page

If I had but two loaves of bread, I would sell one and buy hyacinths, for they would feed my soul.
    The Koran

The Amen! of Nature is always a flower.
    Oliver Wendell Holmes

If you have a garden and a library, you have everything you need.
    Cicero

A bit of fragrance always clings to the hand that gives you roses.
    Chinese Proverb

Sweet flowers are slow and weeds make haste.
    William Shakespeare

Welcome the hope that flowers bring.

The closer you are to the environment the more you come to appreciate it.

The kiss of the sun for - pardon The song of the birds for mirth.
One is nearer God's heart in a garden Than anywhere else on earth.
    Garden Plaque

And the Lord God planted a garden eastward in Eden; and there He put man whom he had formed.
    The Bible - Genesis 2:8

Chapter 5

NO SPRING, NOR SUMMER BEAUTY
HATH SUCH GRACE, AS I HAVE SEEN
IN ONE AUTUMNAL FACE.
JOHN DONNE

The seasons . . . are authentic; there is no mistake about them, they are what a symphony ought to be: four perfect movements in intimate harmony with one another.
    Arthur Rubinstein

If Spring came but once a century instead of once a year, or burst forth with the sound of an earthquake and not in silence, what wonder and expectation there would be in all hearts to behold the miraculous change.
    Henry Wadsworth Longfellow

Came the Spring with all its splendor, all its birds, and all its blossoms, all its flowers, and leaves, and grasses.
    Henry Wadsworth Longfellow

There is no time like Spring, when life's alive in everything.
    Christine Rossetti

The Ides of March have come.
    Julius Caesar

March winds and April showers bring forth May flowers.
    Proverbial Saying

Our Lord has written the promise of the Resurrection, not in books alone, but in every leaf of springtime.
    Martin Luther

Neither Spring, nor Summer beauty hath such grace, As I have seen in one Autumnal face.
    John Donne

Autumn, Oh be less beautiful or be less brief.
    Sir William Watson

Lovely are the silent woods on crisp October days, when the leaves fall red and gold about the quiet ways.
    Patience Strong

Thanksgiving Day is only our annual time for saying grace at the table of eternal goodness.
    James M. Ludlow

The sunshine smiles upon the winter days of my heart, never doubting of its spring flowers.
    Rabindranath Tagore

In the depths of winter, I finally learned that within me there lay an invincible summer.
    Albert Camus

The trumpet of a prophecy! O wind! If Winter comes, can Spring be far behind?
    Percy Bysshe Shelley

Tread lightly, she is near under the snow,
Speak gently, she can hear the daisies grow.
    Oscar Wilde

We must live through the dreary winter If we would value the spring;
And the woods must be cold and silent Before the robins sing.
The flowers must be buried in darkness Before they can bud and bloom,
And the sweetest, warmest sunshine Comes after the storm and gloom.

May the bright spots in the old year be but flickers in the dark when compared with what the New Year will enkindle with its spark.
    Margaret Rorke

Chapter 6

THE HEAVENS DECLARE THE GLORY OF GOD,
THE SKIES PROCLAIM THE WORK OF HIS HANDS.
THE BIBLE - PSALM 19:1

Surely there is something in the unruffled calm of nature that over awes our little anxieties and doubts; the sight of the deep blue sky, and the clustering stars above, seem to impart a quiet to the mind.
    Jonathan Edwards

Every sunrise is a message from God, and every sunset His signature.
    W. A. Ward

The voice of nature loudly cries, and many a message from the skies, that something in us never dies.
    R. Burns

A dream and a star shine best from afar!
    Joan Walsh Anglund

Keep your face to the sunshine and you cannot see the shadow.
    Helen Keller

The world stands out on either side No wider than the heart is wide; Above the world is stretched the sky, No higher than the soul is high.
    Edna St. Vincent Millay

If I shoot at the sun, I may hit a star!
    P. T. Barnum

Hitch your wagon to a star.
    Ralph Waldo Emerson

The same sun that melts the wax hardens the clay.

Day's sweetest moments are at dawn.
    Ella Wheeler Wilcox

My heart leaps up when I behold a rainbow in the sky.
    William Wordsworth

The heavens declare the glory of God; the skies proclaim the work of his hands.
    The Bible - Psalm 19:1 (NIV)

We all live under the same sky, but we don't have the same horizon.
    Konrad Adenauer

Even a small star shines in the darkness.
    Finnish Proverb

Farewell, Morning Star, herald of dawn, and quickly come as the Evening Star, bringing again in secret her whom thou takest away.
    Meleager - 95 BC

More worship the rising than the setting sun.
    Pompey

There is nothing more musical than a sunset.
    Nat Shapero

The more we learn about the wonders of our universe, the more clearly we are going to perceive the hand of God.
    Frank Borman

The moon like a flower in heaven's high bower, with silent delight, sits and smiles on the night.
    William Blake

The man who has seen the rising moon break out of the clouds at midnight has been present like an archangel at the creation of light and of the world.
    Ralph Waldo Emerson

There they stand, the innumerable stars, shining in order like a living hymn, written in light.
    Nathaniel Parker Willis

Chapter 7

**A SMOOTH SEA
NEVER MADE A SKILLFUL MARINER.
ANONYMOUS**

It is not possible to step twice into the same river, for other waters are continually flowing on.
    Heraclitus - 480 BC

Ignore dull days; forget the showers; Keep count of only shining hours.
    German Sundial

We are blessed with the rain as we are with the sun, with the night as with the day.

Rain is God's way of cleansing the earth.
    Carol Maxon Sampson

An hour on a lake is a day in the city.

When you defile the pleasant streams and the wild birds abiding place; you massacre a million dreams and cast your spittle in God's face.
    John Drinkwater

It is the soft but continuous drip of water that will wear away and make an impression on even the hardest rock.

Man wonders over the restless sea . . . the flowing waters . . . the sight of the sky . . . and forgets that of all wonders, man himself is the most wonderful.

My soul is full of longing for the secret of the sea, and the heart of the great ocean sends a thrilling pulse through me.
    Henry Wadsworth Longfellow

Launch out into the deep - let the shoreline go.

A ship is safest in deep water.

A small leak will sink a great ship.

The man who does nothing but wait for his ship to come in has already missed the boat.

The real voyage of discovery consists not in seeking new landscapes but in having new eyes.
    Marcel Proust

It is not the going out of port, but the coming in, that determines the success of a voyage.
    Henry Ward Beecher

A smooth sea never made a skillful mariner.

Give wind and tide a chance to change.

The man who rows the boat doesn't have time to rock it.

Life is not a plateau to be reached, but a river to be sailed.

To be the master of your own ship let your conscience be the compass, and self-discipline the rudder.

We must sail, sometimes with the wind and sometimes against it - but we must sail, and not drift, nor lie at anchor.
    Oliver Wendell Holmes

When you do dance, I wish you a wave o' the sea, that you might ever do nothing but that.
    Shakespeare

You cannot sink someone else's end of the boat and still keep your own afloat.
    Charles Brower

No one would ever have crossed the ocean if he could have gotten off the ship in the storm.

He who will not answer to the rudder must answer to the rocks.

Time and tide wait for no man.
    Geoffrey Chaucer

Time and tide wait for no man, but time always stands still for a woman of thirty.
    Robert Frost

Our plans miscarry because they have no aim. When a man does not know what harbor he is making for, no wind is the right wind.
    Seneca

Anyone can steer the ship when the sea is calm.
    Publilius Syrus

A ship in harbor is safe, but that is not what ships are built for.
    William Shedd

The winds and waves are always on the side of the ablest navigators.
    Edward Gibbon

If you could take the human heart and listen to it, it would be like listening to a seashell, You would hear in it the hollow murmur of the infinite ocean to which it belongs, from which it draws its profoundest inspiration, and for which it yearns.
    Edwin Hubbell Chapin

So I never quite despair, Nor let my courage fail; And some day when skies are fair, Up the bay my ships will sail.
    Robert Barry Coffin

Little boats should keep near shore.
    Benjamin Franklin

Just because the river is quiet, don't think the crocodiles have left.

Over the sea the stork flies. The frog croaks at sunrise. Out to sea the ice flows. Off to plow the farmer goes.
    Folklore

There is a tide in the affairs of men, Which, taken at the flood, leads on to fortune; Omitted, all the voyage of their life Is bound in shallows and in miseries. We must take the current when it serves,
Or lose our ventures.
    William Shakespeare

The power of ideals is incalculable. We see no power in a drop of water. But let it get into a crack in the rock and be turned to ice, and it splits the rock; turned into steam, it drives the pistons of the most powerful engines. Something has happened to it, which makes active and effective the power that is latent in it.
    Albert Schweitzer

No one has a right to live in idleness and expect to live long and be happy. The ship anchored in the harbor rots faster than the ship crossing the ocean; a still pond of water stagnates more rapidly than a running stream. Our unused minds are subject to atrophy much more rapidly than those in use. The unused cells in our brains deteriorate much faster than those, which are continually exercised. Hence, to remain young we must remain active.

I hope my ship comes in before my dock rots.

Chapter 8

**DON'T KNOCK THE WEATHER; NINE-TENTHS OF
THE PEOPLE COULDN'T START A CONVERSATION
IF IT DIDN'T CHANGE ONCE IN A WHILE.
ANONYMOUS**

A rainbow in the morning
Is a shepherd's warning;
But a rainbow at night
Is a shepherd's delight.
    Old Weather Rhyme

Don't knock the weather; nine-tenths of the people couldn't start a conversation if it didn't change once in a while.

Red sky in the morning,
Sailors take warning.
Red sky at night
Sailor's delight.
    Folklore

A sunshiny shower Won't last half an hour.

If a dog or cat sleeps on its back,
There will be rain.

If your shoes squeak or your corns ache, it's going to rain.

Rain before seven,
Quit by eleven;
Thunder before seven,
Rain by eleven.

If it rains on Easter,
It will rain the next six Sundays.

When insects fly low,
A rain will show.

A green Christmas
Means a white Easter.

Plant vegetables and potatoes
On Good Friday.

The bigger the stripes on the caterpillar,
The colder the winter.

When the wind is in the East
Good for neither man nor beast.
When the wind is in the South
Blows the bait in the fish's mouth.
When the wind is in the North
The careful fisherman goes not forth.
When the wind is in the West
That's the time we like it best.

If the wind will not serve, take to the oars.

The winds and waves are always on the side of the ablest navigators.
    Edward Gibbon

Cows lie down when bad weather is coming.

Flowers of the morning glory and scarlet pimpernel open when it's sunny, close when rain is due.

A ring around the moon means rain or snow is coming.

Pine cones close up when rain is on the way.

If a groundhog sees its shadow on Groundhog Day (February 2) the weather will remain cold for six more weeks.

The fog comes on little cat feet.
It sits looking over harbor and city on silent haunches and then moves on.
    Carl Sandburg - 1916

Dandelion petals close when the temperature drops below 50 degrees F.

Dew on grass at night or in early morning is a sign of fair weather.

Birds perch more before storms.

High clouds won't rain on you.

Grasshoppers chirp louder and faster as the temperature rises. Add 37 to the number of chirps in 15 seconds will about equal the temperature.

Seagulls stand facing into the wind so that their feathers won't be ruffled.

Leaves show their backs before rain.

When the air is humid, rain is more likely at low than at high tide.

High visibility over salt water means rain is on the way.

Rising smoke foretells fair weather.

Smells are stronger before rain.

As the air pressure falls, the tissues of the body swell causing pain.

www.ingramcontent.com/pod-product-compliance
Lightning Source LLC
LaVergne TN
LVHW061935070526
838199LV00060B/3836